Pandora's Jukebox

Fifty-two recording artists to teach your kids

Craig Trembirth

Copyright © Craig Trembirth (2024)

First edition

No part of this book may be reproduced or transmitted by any means, except as permitted by UK copyright law or the author. For licensing requests, please contact the author at craig.trembirth@gmail.com.

Cover design by Scott Hingley, Touch Design
www.touchdesign.co.uk

For Adam and Molly

Contents

2	About this book	109	PJ Harvey
3	Parental guidance	113	Housemartins/Beautiful South
5	808 State	117	Hüsker Dü
9	Aaliyah	121	The Jam
13	Air	125	Joy Division
17	Alabama Shakes	129	The Kinks
21	Tori Amos	133	Kraftwerk
25	The Avalanches	137	Lady Gaga
29	BABYMETAL	141	Little Richard
33	Bee Gees	145	Lizzo
37	Björk	149	Mazzy Star
41	Blondie	153	Missy Elliott
45	Kate Bush	157	Nirvana
49	Johnny Cash	161	Sinéad O'Connor
53	Tracy Chapman	165	Dolly Parton
57	Chic	169	Portishead
61	Norman Cook	173	The Prodigy
65	Daft Punk	177	Minnie Riperton
69	Depeche Mode	181	Robyn
73	Delia Derbyshire	185	Sigur Rós
77	The Doors	189	Nina Simone
81	Billie Eilish	193	Dusty Springfield
85	Elastica	197	The Strokes
89	The Fall	201	Sister Rosetta Tharpe
93	Florence + the Machine	205	Toots and the Maytals
97	Fugees	209	Amy Winehouse
101	John Grant	214	Acknowledgements
105	Groove Armada	215	Also by the author

About this book

The weekly trip to the running club with my nephew coincides with the radio station playing their Album of the Week. I was amazed as to how few of the artists Adam knew as I thought his dad (my brother) would introduce him and his sister, Molly, to the music we listened to growing up. I went in search of a book featuring bands and musicians to teach your kids about, but there wasn't one, so I've written it.

The book highlights fifty-two influential recording artists – one for your own Album of the Week. The list is far from definitive and I've deliberately left out the biggest names – if you haven't brought your children up without at least a glimpse of Bowie, the Beatles, Prince etc. then no book in the world is going to help you! Some have been influential in the development of music while others have used their platform to raise awareness of important issues.

Now it's over to you – Grab your kids or nudge your adults and use this book as a signpost to the bands and musicians to embark on your own journey of appreciation and love (or otherwise) of the music that has been created.

Join the conversation

What did you make of the fifty-two that made the cut? Who do you think is worthy of inclusion next time? Has the book introduced you to anyone new? Join in the conversation and share your experiences:

- Pandora's Jukebox - 52
- #pandorasjukebox52

The playlist

Let's be honest, who wants to read about music when you can spend time sitting back and listening to it? I've created a playlist of all the singles featured in the book along with a few bonus tracks. You can find it by scanning the QR code (right).

Parental guidance

The book's intention is that you make your way through it with your children and therefore it's only fair that you get a heads-up as to where there are either explicit lyrics or references to less salubrious activity. You may want to check these out in advance and make a decision as to how you approach them with your kids:

- Aaliyah – Illegal marriage and underage sex.
- Alabama Shakes – Child abuse.
- Avalanches – Explicit previous band name.
- Norman Cook – An explicit song title.
- Depeche Mode – Drug use.
- The Doors – Drug use.
- Hüsker Dü – Drug use.
- Joy Division – Sexual slavery.
- Sinéad O'Connor – Sexual abuse.
- Amy Winehouse – Drug use.

While I've tried to find the radio edit versions of the tracks for the playlist, singles and albums containing explicit lyrics have been marked in the book with [E].

PARENTAL ADVISORY EXPLICIT CONTENT

808 State

808 State was formed by the trio of Graham Massey, Martin Price and Gerald Simpson in Manchester in 1987. Their early work in particular had a massive influence on the UK acid house genre and the subsequent sound of techno and intelligent dance music. They were also early pioneers in the Madchester scene, which saw lads start dancing together in clubs rather than beating each other up on the football terraces. Their innovative approach to production, fearless exploration of genres and ability to fuse different musical elements continue to inspire artists decades later.

The group's name derives from the Roland TR-808 drum machine, which was the go-to instrument in the development of electronic music during the late 1980s. The machine is synonymous with its distinctive, deep, whale-like bass tones and booming kicks that became iconic elements of the 808 State sound.

In 1988 the band released their debut album *Newbuild* on Price's own record label. The record showcased their unique blend of electronic music styles that included acid house, techno and ambient with tracks including "Flow Coma" and "Let Yourself Go" featuring the band's distinctive beats, abstract synths and innovative use of samples.

808 State's style was epitomised a year later with the release of "Pacific State". With its blend of infectious melody and percussion, the single became synonymous with the band and an anthem of the era.

Similar artists:

The Future Sound of London
The Orb
Orbital
The Shamen

"Pacific State" was picked up by Radio 1 DJ Gary Davies although rumours that he referred to the band as "Bob State" on *Top of the Pops* are unfortunately untrue. The subsequent success propelled the group to mainstream attention and earned them a devoted following with the single charting for eleven weeks in the UK, peaking at Number 10. After this success, however, founder member Gerald Simpson left the group to become known as A Guy Called Gerald.

808 State released the mini-album *Quadrastate* in July 1989, followed less than six months later by full album *90* in December the same year. Featuring the aforementioned "Pacific State" the album peaked at Number 57. The following year saw the band collaborate with MC Tunes on his album *The North at Its Heights*, which reached Number 26 and included the Top 10 hit "The Only Rhyme That Bites".

Greater success was to come with the fourth album, *ex:el*, peaking at Number 4. The band recruited the vocals of Björk, who was still with the Sugarcubes at the time, as well as Joy Division/New Order's Bernard Sumner, demonstrating a willingness to collaborate and a desire to explore new sounds. The album yielded two Top 10 singles, "Cubik/Olympic" and "In Yer Face". At this time Massey was also a member of a band called Aqua, however, they're not to be confused with the Europop band of the same name and he is in no way responsible for the 1997 novelty single "Barbie Girl".

Singled out:

"Pacific State" – A perfect percussion for the clubs of Manchester with a wistfully synthesised wind instrument that makes you dream that you're anywhere other than in Manchester.

"Qmart" – An eccentric collaboration with Björk that is so synonymous with both band and singer that it appears like a baby in which you can see the features of both parents.

"The Only Rhyme That Bites" – A joyful mix of heroic rap and epic movie soundtrack, created with MC Tunes and sampling *The Big Country* theme to make a big Top 10 hit.

New members Andy Barker and Darren Partington joined the fray in 1989 while Price left the group in 1991. 1993's album, *Gorgeous*, reached the Top 20 and the collaborations continued, none larger than working with David Bowie on a remix of "Sound and Vision".

Further collaborations included James Dean Bradfield from the Manic Street Preachers on their 1996 album *Don Solaris* with the resulting single "Lopez" reaching Number 20. Elbow's Guy Garvey then appeared, among others, on the 2002 album *Outpost Transmission*.

In 2015 Partington left the band after being given a jail sentence, leaving Massey and Barker to produce 2019's *Transmission Suite* seventeen years after their previous album. Two years later Andy Barker passed away after a short illness.

Album of the week: *ex:el*

808's fourth album was more accessible than previous offerings and one of those equally at home at an illegal rave or middle-class dinner party. The more palatable nature led to the LP becoming the band's only Top 10 album at a time when electronic dance music was encroaching into the charts.

Bands including the Shamen and KLF were poking the mainstream while *ex:el* peaked at Number 4, spawning two Top 10 singles "Cubik/Olympic" and "In Yer Face".

The album was one of the first to use alternative artists to feature in the songs, in this case Joy Division/New Order's Bernard Sumner and the Sugarcubes' Björk, prior to her going solo. This saw the start of a long-term collaboration between Graham Massey and the Icelandic superstar (that's Björk, not fellow Mancunian Sumner).

The album was also the first to sample the phrase, "We are the music makers" from *Charlie and the Chocolate Factory* in the fifth track "Nephatiti", which soon became a key ingredient to many electronic albums from then on.

Since their inception towards the end of the 1980s, 808 State have consistently evolved and adapted to changing musical landscapes while maintaining their distinctive sound. Beyond their studio albums they delivered energetic and immersive live shows that combined DJing, live instrumentation and incredible visuals, creating a multi-sensory experience that left a lasting impact on those lucky enough to witness them.

Your thoughts and reviews:

☆ ☆ ☆ ☆ ☆

Aaliyah

In her short but impactful career, Aaliyah left an indelible mark on the world of R&B and pop music. Her stuttering, futuristic style, which infused pop, electro, hip-hop and funk helped to redefine contemporary R&B from the mid-1990s and saw it cross into the mainstream. Aaliyah paved the way for artists who imitated her style including Alicia Keys, Christina Aguilera and Destiny's Child (and therefore two hundred million-record-selling Beyoncé).

Aaliyah Dana Haughton, who dropped her surname on the advice of her mother, was born in Brooklyn, New York, in 1979. Such was her command of her genre she soon became known as the Princess of R&B and the Queen of Urban Pop, depending on which royal family you bow to.

Her first taste of fame was at the age of ten when she appeared on US TV's *Star Search*, a precursor to *Britain's Got Talent* but with a history of unearthing future celebrities that include Justin Timberlake, Beyoncé, Britney Spears, Alanis Morissette, Christina Aguilera and Sinbad (that's the comedian, not the sailor).

Aaliyah signed her first record deal at the age of twelve while working with her uncle, Barry Hankerson. Hankerson was an entertainment lawyer and former husband of Gladys Knight but this was far from a case of nepotism with Knight confident enough with the young singer to have her appearing with her on a tour, which included five nights in Las Vegas.

Similar artists:

Ashanti
Destiny's Child
Monica
SWV

Aaliyah released her debut album *Age Ain't Nothing but a Number* in 1994 when she was just fifteen. It sold three million copies in the US and six million copies worldwide while debut single "Back & Forth" peaked at Number 16 in the UK. Further singles "At Your Best (You Are Love)", "Age Ain't Nothing but a Number" and "Down with the Clique" all reached the Top 40. The album was later shadowed however after allegations emerged of an illegal marriage between Aaliyah and the record's producer and songwriter R Kelly.

Aaliyah therefore left Jive Records, signing for Atlantic Records and forming an even more potent partnership with Missy Elliott and Timbaland for her second studio album *One in a Million*. The album spawned two Top 20 singles, "If Your Girl Only Knew" and title track "One in a Million", both of which showcased her ability to combine infectious melodies and soulful lyrics. The album went on to sell more than eight million copies worldwide.

As well as blending musical genres, Aaliyah also combined her career in music with a talent for acting. In first grade she was cast in *Annie* and later sang "Ave Maria" entirely in Italian as part of her audition for the Detroit High School for the Fine and Performing Arts. This paved the way for roles as Trish O'Day in 1999's *Romeo Must Die* and Akasha in 2002's *Queen of the Damned*. However, while hugely successful this somewhat placed an obstacle to her next album *Aaliyah*, which took five years to complete, eventually being released in July 2001 and peaking at Number 5.

Singled out:

- "More Than a Woman" – The contrast of staccato hip-hop slipping into the soulful pop chorus blends the two genres into a combination as delightful as jelly and ice cream.

- "Try Again" – Impossible to listen to without conjuring up "Independent Woman" by Destiny's Child, released seven months later, highlighting Aaliyah's indelible influence on the industry.

- "One in a Million" – Showcasing Aaliyah's incredible voice, where the vocal soars and falls like those starling murmurations off Brighton Pier.

Tragically, just over one month after the release of album *Aaliyah* the singer, along with all passengers, was killed in a plane crash after filming the video for "Rock the Boat". She was just twenty-two years old.

Posthumous singles "More Than a Woman" and "Rock the Boat" reached Number 1 and Number 12 respectively while the album went on to sell over thirteen million copies worldwide. Subsequent releases have continued to enhance Aaliyah's legacy and in December 2002 compilation album *I Care 4 U*, containing a number of singles and previously unreleased recordings, peaked at Number 4 although only the single "Don't Know What to Tell Ya" troubled the upper echelons of the chart, peaking at Number 22.

Album of the week: *Aaliyah*

Aaliyah started work on this, her final album, in 1998 but had to balance her burgeoning acting career alongside the music. She recorded tracks in the evening after filming for *Queen of the Damned* in the day, hence the delay.

Initially the album sold well, which is unsurprising when you consider the collaborators included Missy Elliott, Timbaland and main songwriter, Static (while a partnership with Trent Reznor failed to materialise).

Legal conflicts meant the album took twenty years before landing on streaming platforms but with its effortless blend of R&B, soul, funk, hip-hop and Latin music it still feels as fresh as when it was released.

The album finally emerged at a time when R&B was in the ascendency – Destiny's Child had hit Number 1 around the world with "Survivor" in April the same year *Aaliyah* was released.

Sadly Aaliyah died in a plane crash on returning from filming the video to promote "Rock the Boat". After this, the fourth track "More Than a Woman" hit the Number 1 slot.

The album eventually peaked at Number 5 in the UK in 2002 and sold over thirteen million copies worldwide.

Aaliyah's final release was the 2005 box set *Ultimate Aaliyah*, which contained three discs. The first is a greatest hits collection containing no less than sixteen songs while disc 2 featured material from the many soundtracks that the singer contributed to. These include her Number 5 hit single "Try Again" from the *Romeo Must Die* soundtrack. Songs from Timbaland's studio albums also appear while the third disc chronicles a documentary of her life.

In the decades since her death, Aaliyah's music has continued to influence artists across the world and has sold in excess of thirty-two million albums.

Your thoughts and reviews:

☆☆☆☆☆

Air

Air is an absolute treat from Versailles who heavily influenced the genre of electronic music. They incorporated a wide variety of instruments and sounds, from vintage synthesizers and drum machines to live strings and horns, as well as recruiting guest vocalists to perform. Synonymous with a dreamy, ethereal aesthetic, the band has been instrumental in shaping how the English-speaking world, still hung up on Sacha Distel, conceives French music.

Air was created following Nicolas Godin and Jean-Benoît Dunckel's meeting while Godin was studying architecture and Dunckel read mathematics, as they say on *University Challenge*. The pair shared a common interest in music and quickly formed a friendship, initially working with others as part of the band Orange but soon peeled away and sublimated to form Air.

Some people believe Air to be an acronym for amour, imagination, and rêve, which translates as love, imagination, and dreaming but this has been disputed. It would certainly help in making a distinction between Godin playing AIR guitar rather than playing air guitar though.

The duo never confined themselves to keyboards and used a variety of instruments, often improvising when playing live to produce extended versions of their established songs. This experimental approach saw even their most recognisable songs evolve over time, adding to the ethereal quality in which you knew what to expect yet still left feeling you'd been offered more.

Similar artists:

Goldfrapp
Lamb
Röyksopp
Zero 7

After spending their initial years remixing other songs Air shot to fame upon releasing debut album *Moon Safari* in 1998. The album also launched the career of Beth Hirsch, who was a neighbour of Godin, in the process. The album reached Number 6 in the UK with debut single "Sexy Boy" peaking at number 13. Other singles "Kelly Watch the Stars" and "All I Need", with vocals by Hirsch, peaked at Numbers 18 and 29 respectively.

The band's dreamy, cinematic style was little heard of outside of dreams and the cinema and added a certain je ne sais quoi to what was being played at the time. It was no surprise that their follow-up to *Moon Safari* was the film soundtrack to *The Virgin Suicides*, a 1999 American psychological drama written and directed by Sofia Coppola, which reached Number 14. They would later go on to produce the film score for Georges Méliès' *Le Voyage Dans La Lune* in 2012.

In between, Air produced a further four studio albums each exploring new sonic territories while maintaining their signature fragile quality. 2001's *10 000 Hz Legend* saw similar success to *Moon Safari*, peaking at Number 7, but of the four singles released only "Radio #1" troubled the charts, peaking at Number 31.

The band's next offering was a remix album of tracks from *10 000 Hz Legend*, five of which were alternatives to the track "Don't Be Light". Released in 2002 they entitled the collection *Everybody Hertz* (see what they did there?).

Singled out:

"Cherry Blossom Girl" – Jean-Benoît Dunckel's voice adds a layer of seduction to Air's brand of futuristic electronica that you could imagine Buck Rogers hosting dinner parties to.

"Kelly Watch the Stars" – Written about *Charlie's Angels'* Kelly Garrett, this is a cacophony of incessant bass accompanied by intergalactic swirls, ethereal whistles and a rollercoaster piano.

"Playground Love" – Simply delicious, emitting the same feeling as when, after a long journey, your train pulls into a railway station where you know your lover is waiting.

Air's otherworldly soundscapes are perfect for setting the stylus to the start of an entire album, letting it play out and drifting on the lilting sounds as they envelop a darkened room, kind of like we did before streaming became the norm.

In 2004 the band released their standout album *Talkie Walkie*, which reached Number 2. While the single "Cherry Blossom Girl" failed to hit the Top 100 in the UK it did chart highly on the US Dance Sales Chart, as did "Surfing on a Rocket", which reached the Top 50 in the US. Single "Alpha Beta Gaga" did at least chart in the UK albeit a relatively lowly 44.

The band followed this with *Pocket Symphony* in 2007 when, in a move away from their French routes they sought contributions from Jarvis Cocker of Pulp and Neil Hannon from the Divine Comedy, who couldn't have been more English if they'd hired Winston Churchill and William Shakespeare. Meanwhile Godin began playing Japanese instruments including the koto and the shamisen.

Album of the week: *Talkie Walkie*

Air's third studio album, a Number 2 hit, showed the French disco sensations could walkie the walkie as well as talkie the talkie. The pair weren't trying to be clever though as talkie walkie is literally French for walkie talkie.

The album was as ethereal and cinematic as ever, and it's no surprise that the final track "Alone in Kyoto" was used in the film *Lost in Translation* while the third track "Run" was used in *Lila Says* and an episode of *Veronica Mars*.

Uncharacteristically (if you can have developed a character only three albums in) the duo did away with guest vocalists, playing and singing every note themselves. You can't help but think that Hope Sandoval's involvement in remixing "Cherry Blossom Girl" without contributing her unique voice could be the biggest lost opportunity in French history since their men's football team failed to qualify for the 1994 World Cup though.

Album *Love 2*, tantalisingly hinting that there's a lost album called *Love 1* somewhere out there, was released in 2009 and peaked at Number 36. This was followed by the aforementioned *Le Voyage Dans La Lune*. The band's final release came in 2014 when they were commissioned by the Palais des Beaux-Arts de Lille to record nine-track, sixty-nine-minute, *Music for Museum*. However, only one thousand copies were printed, on translucent vinyl no less, so it's clear to see why this one failed to chart.

Your thoughts and reviews:

☆ ☆ ☆ ☆ ☆

Alabama Shakes

Alabama Shakes' impact on the music industry extends far beyond their own relatively limited discography. They have inspired a new generation of artists, proving that authenticity and soul can still thrive in a world dominated by manufactured pop acts. Their success has paved the way for a resurgence of soulful, guitar-driven rock music reminding listeners of the power of a well-crafted song and a captivating performance.

Alabama Shakes formed in the world's second most famous Athens in 2009. The band, consisting of lead singer and guitarist Brittany Howard, guitarist Heath Fogg, bassist Zac Cockrell and drummer Steve Johnson certainly worked their way into the ears of the music-loving public the hard way.

Howard taught herself, along with local kids in the community, how to play the guitar as well as the drums and bass during a troubled childhood, which included the death of her sister. Once together, the band toured bars and clubs for two years before putting their first record together, achieved while still unsigned. Online popularity brought them to the attention of ATO Records who signed the band and released that first album.

During the time of relative obscurity, the band members all had other day jobs, which included Howard being employed as a postal worker and a chef while other members had roles including painter and decorator, vet and even taking shifts at the Browns Ferry nuclear power plant.

Similar artists:

Liam Bailey
The Black Keys
Edward Sharpe and the Magnetic Zeroes
St Paul and the Broken Bones

Howard met Fogg in junior high school and bassist Zac Cockrell in a psychology class sometime later. Zac suggested to Steve Johnson that he should attend Howard's twice-weekly jam sessions at her great-grandparents' home. Without Fogg, the three began making music together and recording homemade demos with Fogg jumping on the bandwagon after their live debut in 2009.

Their early sound was said to borrow much from mid-20th century rhythm and blues and is indicative of the area of the southern United States from where they hail. Their sound, along with Howard's voice, has been compared to artists such as Janis Joplin while Howard herself has stated that her inspiration came more from the soulful singing of Bon Scott of AC/DC.

Originally called just the Shakes the band had to change or at least adapt their name once fame beckoned. After putting a request out on Facebook for suggestions they eventually just added the Alabama bit and the rest is history (and a bit of geography).

They released their debut album *Boys & Girls* in 2012, which peaked at Number 3 in the UK and Number 6 in their native US where it has sold more than one million records. The album coincided with their status as being the must-see band at festivals across the UK, which added to the group's reputation. A year later they played for Barack and Michelle Obama at the White House and also at the Grammys.

Singled out:

"Gimme All Your Love" – The only single released in the UK, it's raw and shouty, tender as a rare steak then concludes with a funky sprint finish a bit like a sports massage.

"Hold On" – Sounding like every musician involved brought their A-game to the table, and the chairs and every other piece of furniture into the studio. At just 3:46 it implores an encore.

"Miss You" – Unapologetically bluesy with powerful vocals that are both controlled yet so totally out of control, this may also be the only song ever to reference the Honda Accord.

In 2015 the band released their second studio album *Sound & Color*. The music was more eclectic and steeped in several genres including elements of psychedelia, funk and R&B. The album peaked at Number 6 and heralded the band's only UK chart hit "Gimme All Your Love", which just crept in at Number 97.

Alabama Shakes are known for their raw energy and emotional intensity. Howard's powerful vocals and Fogg's intricate guitar combined to create an immersive sound while their high-energy shows were one of the main reasons behind the band's rise to stardom. This is mostly down to Howard, whose performances evoked memories of iconic female vocalists such as Sister Rosetta Tharpe, Aretha Franklin and Tina Turner.

The band has also used their platform to raise awareness of social and political issues with Howard in particular speaking out about racial inequality, LGBTQ+ rights and other causes important to them.

Album of the week: *Boys & Girls*

Debut albums don't come much better than this, soaring beautifully to Number 3 upon its April release like the summer rising from months of a bitter winter.

The blues-based rock album offers quick snippets of their undoubted talent. With only two of the songs lasting in excess of four minutes and four less than three, the thirty-six minutes end before you realise how fantastic they are.

While a similar sound of bands and musicians such as the Black Keys and Jack White became revered (the latter's *Blunderbus* hit Number 1 the same month *Boys & Girls* was released, and they did get to go on tour with him), singles "Hold On", "I Ain't the Same" and "Hang Loose" criminally failed to chart.

One of the main appeals of this album is that Brittany Howard's voice resonates with such emotion. What makes it even better is that it's not entirely clear what that emotion is.

In 2018 the band went on a hiatus due to Howard's focus on solo projects, which led her to tour in 2019. She has since gone on to be a member of bands with names including Thunderbitch and Bermuda Triangle. In June 2020 guitarist Heath Fogg also released a debut solo project while Steven Johnson's trajectory has proved far less salubrious.

Your thoughts and reviews:

Tori Amos

Known for her distinctive and powerful voice, evocative lyrics and virtuosic piano playing, Tori Amos has released sixteen studio albums each showcasing her evolution as an artist in a career spanning four decades. She has also been an outspoken advocate for women's rights and uses her platform to address social and political issues, becoming the first spokesperson for America's Rape, Abuse & Incest National Network (RAINN) in 1994.

Born Myra Ellen Amos in the summer of 1963, Tori Amos performed under her middle name Ellen up until 1980. Thereafter she adopted Tori after a friend's boyfriend told her she looked like a Torrey pine tree.

Amos taught herself how to play the piano at the age of two and composed her first tunes at the age of three. At home she would play songs by the Beatles and the Doors but in a classical style so her father, a minister, wouldn't know that she was playing what he called Devil's music.

At the age of five Amos won a scholarship to the Peabody Institute at Johns (yes, the 's' should be there) Hopkins University, joining their preparatory division where she lasted six years before being asked to leave due to her reluctance to read music. She describes seeing music as structures of light, similar to chromesthesia where sound evokes an experience of colour, shape, and movement, and therefore the decision was mutual as she felt the institute was stifling this creative side of her.

Similar artists:

10,000 Maniacs
Kate Bush
Aimee Mann
Suzanne Vega

After several years performing in local gay bars and piano bars in Maryland, Amos moved to Los Angeles in 1984 to further pursue her music career. In 1986 she formed a musical group with the self-depreciatingly named Y Kant Tori Read but following the failure of their only album, which Amos herself has criticised, the group disbanded.

Despite the disappointment Amos had to comply with a six-record contract and so released debut *Little Earthquakes* in 1992. The album was a greater success, reaching Number 14 and selling over three million copies worldwide.

Her second album *Under the Pink* reached Number 1 in 1994, helped along by the Number 4 hit single "Cornflake Girl" (nobody knew what the title meant, we just hoped she wouldn't fall victim to a cereal killer). The album was followed by *Boys for Pele*, released in 1996, which peaked at Number 2. "Caught a Lite Sneeze" was the first single release streamed prior to an album while the record was further bolstered by the single "Professional Widow". Remixed by American DJ, Armand van Helden and released in the UK as "Professional Widow (It's Got to Be Big)", the single hit the Number 1 slot and remains one of the most recognisable dance tracks of all time.

At this time Amos was trying to distance herself from her record company and so recorded *Boys for Pele* in a church in County Wicklow, Ireland. The move paid off and therefore she went on to have the barn of her adoptive home in Cornwall converted to a recording studio for future work.

Singled out:

"Cornflake Girl" – Exemplifying Tori Amos's swirling piano and sublime vocals the bonus is being asked if this is one of your favourite songs and being able to reply, "You bet your life it is!"

"Strange Little Girl" – Originally a hit for the Stranglers, Amos's female vocal lends a completely different, almost introspective focus to the lyrics.

"Professional Widow (It's Got to Be Big)" [E] – A defining dance track of the 1990s, it's nothing like the original yet captures the same theme of female desire that Amos never avoided.

The singer's next album, 1998's *From the Choirgirl Hotel*, also reached the Top 10 while 1999's *To Venus and Back* peaked at Number 22. Both saw a move away from her trademark acoustic, piano-based sound to be replaced by electronica and dance music. Her subsequent album *Strange Little Girls*, created shortly after giving birth to her daughter, was a cover album that took songs written by men about women, such as the Velvet Underground's "New Age" and Eminem's "97 Bonnie & Clyde" and reversed the gender roles.

Amos released a further ten studio albums with varying degrees of commercial success. *Abnormally Attracted to Sin* (2009), *Unrepentant Geraldines* (2014) and *Native Invader* (2017) all reached the Top 20 in the UK. She released her sixteenth and most recent album *Ocean to Ocean* in 2021, written during and inspired somewhat by lockdown from the Covid-19 pandemic while also taking inspiration from the stunning landscapes and ancient myths of her adoptive Cornwall to produce the record, which peaked at Number 25.

Album of the week: *Under the Pink*

Buoyed by the success of Top 5 hit "Cornflake Girl", released prior to the album, *Under the Pink* entered the UK Charts at Number 1, selling over three hundred thousand copies in the UK while eventually selling over two million copies in her native US.

Single "Pretty Good Year" was also a Top 10 hit while other tracks "God" and "Past the Mission" fared less well, despite the latter featuring Trent Reznor on backing vocals.

The album was a triumph and was the perfect aftershock to debut *Little Earthquakes* with critics fearing (or some secretly hoping) that Amos would be unable to live up to her initial success.

With cryptic lyrics covering themes including religion, gender and sexuality, along with an undercurrent of how women treat each other in a patriarchal society, there were more than a few mouths agape once we realised what Tori Amos was actually singing about.

She spent 2023 on tour finally getting to promote *Ocean to Ocean* after previous dates were postponed due to the pandemic.

Her flame-red hair makes Tori Amos one of the most distinctive musicians in history while her lyrics recount her religious upbringing, sexual awakening, identity, gender and desires. Her debut album indicated that she would not shy away from taboo subjects, including personal and introspective themes of femininity and spirituality that have brought her a huge following along with great success.

Your thoughts and reviews:

The Avalanches

The Avalanches are known for their unique blend of sample-based music, which incorporates elements of hip-hop, dance and pop. Formed in the late 1990s, they are widely regarded as one of the best bands of the plunderphonics genre – the style consisting of music made either predominantly or completely of sampling recognisable musical works, educational films, news reports, radio shows, or anything with trained vocal announcers.

The Avalanches formed in Melbourne, Australia, in 1997. Current members Robbie Chater and Tony Di Blasi, along with Darren Seltmann (who would leave the band in 2006) had formed noise-punk outfit Alarm 115 three years previous although the group had to disband when drummer Manabu Etoh was deported.

As well as instruments and recording gear the group had bought a number of old vinyl records. These became the core feature of a new project that saw Chater and Seltmann create a thirty-minute demo from the records. Needing a group to play the tracks live, Chater and Seltmann brought in old bandmate Di Blasi along with Gordon McQuilten.

The band played under various names throughout 1997, which included Quentin's Brittle Bones and the Swinging Monkey Cocks. They finally settled on the less controversial Avalanches, which they took from an American surf-rock band, who'd released a single album *Ski Surfin'* in the early 1960s.

Similar artists:

2 Many DJs
LCD Soundsystem
Lemon Jelly
DJ Shadow

In 1997 the Avalanches released their debut single "Rock City" from the EP *El Producto*, although this is unlikely to be about the legendary concert venue in Nottingham. Around this time the group were joined by DJ Dexter Fabay and James Dela Cruz while their profile was growing significantly with high-profile slots supporting bands including the Beastie Boys, Public Enemy and Beck.

The band started recording their debut album *Since I Left You* in 1998 and eventually finished the project in early 2000. The release was initially delayed however over the need for sample clearances with founder member Chater estimating that approximately three and a half thousand samples were used.

The album was launched in Melbourne with a boat party although it wasn't all plain sailing for the band, with Seltmann breaking his leg in an on-stage collision with Di Blasi while on tour promoting the album. The promotion also included a three-week stint in the UK, which included DJ sets at the Social and Fabric nightclubs.

Since I Left You had a staggered release across the world from late 2000 and into 2001. It was released in the UK in April 2001, peaking at Number 8 and selling over two hundred thousand records in the process. Singles "Frontier Psychiatrist" and "Since I Left You" both reached the Top 20. The videos were also lauded with the former awarded the runner-up prize at the Soho Shorts Film Festival while the latter won Video of the Year at the MTV Europe Music Awards.

Singled out:

- "Frontier Psychiatrist" – Demonstrating the band's ability to make cohesive musical sense out of an ensemble of vocal and orchestral samples, this track is both astonishing and somewhat hilarious.

- "Since I Left You" – Featuring a prominent vocal sample of "Everyday" by the Main Attraction, this gives the same feeling as waking up thinking it's a workday only to realise it's the weekend.

- "The Divine Chord" – This collaboration with rock royalty Johnny Marr and MGMT proved that the band could create the same uplifting tunes without using other peoples' work as samples.

The band started work on their second album in 2005 but it would take over eleven years to release, largely due to Darren Seltmann leaving the group and Robbie Chater having to deal with two separate auto-immune diseases. They eventually released *Wildfire* in July 2016 and saw it peak at Number 10.

The wait for their next album was a little shorter with *We Will Always Love You* released in December 2020. The album, which peaked at Number 39 in the UK but secured a Top 5 slot in their native Australia features contributions from artists including MGMT, Tricky, Neneh Cherry, Jamie xx and Mick Jones of the Clash.

Album of the week: *Since I Left You*

Without thinking that this album would be anything special the Avalanches forged ahead, sampling willy-nilly without thinking about the consequences.

This approach may have been ok if they'd stuck to more obscure samples but nicking the bassline of Madonna's "Holiday" raised the LP's prominence with all the triumph of Jaws emerging on the shores of Amity Island.

The resultant requests and gaining permissions delayed the album for a couple of years although the adjournment was well worth the wait.

The outcome was an LP that peaked at Number 8 and Number 5 in their native Australia, spawning two Top 20 singles in "Frontier Psychiatrist" and "Since I Left You". Meanwhile the brilliant seventeenth track "Live at Dominoes", if released, could've easily propelled the Avalanches into territory inhabited by the likes of Daft Punk and Groove Armada.

As they experimented with the plunderphonics genre the voices of scientists in their many samples may have been a subconscious act, however, what emerged was a unique sound that conjures up thoughts of those innocent yet bonkers Saturday mornings just spent watching cartoons.

The Avalanches are widely regarded as one of the pioneers of the plunderphonics genre with the album *Since I Left You* sandwiched between DJ Shadow's *Endtroducing* (1996) and J Dilla's *Donuts* (2006) as exemplars of the music. Meanwhile their final album demonstrates their willingness to move away from this genre to prove they could also forge their own sound in their own way.

Your thoughts and reviews:

☆ ☆ ☆ ☆ ☆

BABYMETAL

BABYMETAL are an entirely new phenomenon and might be a band your kids end up teaching *you* about. Hailing from Japan they present a unique and groundbreaking sound that merges heavy metal and J-pop to create the kawaii metal genre. They have since gone on to global fame, taking Japanese music into uncharted territories outside of their native Asia while using their platform to focus on positivity and self-empowerment, in particular the body image concerns of girls and women.

BABYMETAL was formed in 2010 with original members Suzuka Nakamoto as Su-metal, Moa Kikuchi as Moametal and Yui Mizuno as Yuimetal. Su-metal's role is vocal and dance while the other members scream and dance.

The band started as a sub-unit of the group Sakura Gakuin but became independent when, not unlike that scene from *Logan's Run* where everyone over the age of thirty gets euthanised, Nakamoto graduated from junior high school and therefore became unable to perform for a group made up solely of elementary and junior high school pupils.

The band's self-styled kawaii metal genre seamlessly fuses heavy guitar riffs, pounding drums and aggressive yet joyful vocals with catchy melodies. Wade in with some uplifting choruses and synchronized dance routines and you have a sound and aesthetic that is both heavy and melodic while aggressive and accessible.

Similar artists:

ATARASHI GAKKO!
BAND-MAID
Kikuo
PassCode

The band's eponymous debut album was released in 2014 and sold over thirty-seven thousand copies in its first week in their native Japan while landing just outside the Top 100 in the UK. Their music quickly spread and topped the iTunes Metal Charts in the UK, Germany and the US.

Relative celebrity brought them to the attention of the Fame Monster herself with Lady Gaga adopting them as support during her *ArtRave: The Artpop Ball* tour in the US throughout that same year. Meanwhile their own world tour included a night at the Brixton Academy while a fan-led campaign put them on the bill at the heavy metal Sonisphere Festival.

The following year they played the Reading/Leeds Festival and went on to play Download in 2016. This coincided with the release of their second album *Metal Resistance*, which peaked at Number 15. At the time it was the highest-ever chart entry for a Japanese band while in April they became the first Japanese band to headline Wembley Arena, which resulted in the largest-ever sale of merchandise inside the arena and probably outside on the pavements too as Del Boyesque bootleggers cashed in with T-shirts for a fiver.

Their live schedule didn't abate while their degrees of separation within the rock world diminished, with an itinerary including support slots for the Red Hot Chilli Peppers, and Metallica and Guns N' Roses the following year. In 2018 they returned to Download, which was a triumph after the festival's organisers had previously vowed never to have them on the bill at all.

Singled out:

"Gimme Chocolate!!" – Relying on YouTube hits and streaming alone, this track with its ridiculous BPM is a mash of thrash metal and 1980s arcade game mixed with a hint of "Crazy Frog".

"Headbangeeeeerrrrr!!!!!" – Suzuka Nakamoto's precise vocals carry this epic track like an ancient Oriental battle cry rising over a sea of sword-wielding infantry.

"Karate" – I would spend a decade replacing the most well-known scores from John Williams with this track just to elevate every single film he wrote the music to.

Yui Mizuno decided to leave the band in 2018 citing poor health but the band continued. In 2019 they released their third album *Metal Galaxy*, which again hit the UK's Top 20. With it they continued to evolve the kawaii sound, employing instruments from a variety of countries they had encountered throughout previous world tours and exploring the idea of cultural diversity that this embracing would bring. That year they broke new ground again by becoming the first Japanese band to play one of the main stages at the Glastonbury Festival.

The group added to their number in 2023 when they were joined by Momoko Okazaki, another former member of Sakura Gakuin. Under the stage name Momometal, Okazaki brought the group back up to a trio in time for their fourth album *The Other One*. The album was released in March and peaked at Number 32 while securing a fourth successive Top 5 hit album in their native Japan.

Album of the week: *Metal Resistance*

Proving their debut album was far from a fad the band attempted and succeeded in building a bridge with their audience with more uplifting lyrics while reaching into other genres of music.

This included a distinctive drum and bass introduction to the third track "Awadama Fever" and the tenth track "No Rain, No Rainbow", which would be at home at any Eurovision Song Contest over the previous ten years.

Their first track sung in English, "The One", also looked to expand their appeal.

The album, which was released in Japanese format in their native land and another for the rest of the world, peaked at Number 15 in the UK – the highest ever achieved by a Japanese band while they played the iconic Wembley Arena less than a week after its release.

With soaring female vocals placed upon the heavy metal background, somewhat reminiscent of Evanescence, the result is an hour of genre-busting sound that shouldn't work but clearly does.

On their way to global stardom, BABYMETAL has broken cultural barriers and introduced a new generation of music fans to the world of heavy metal, all while challenging preconceived notions of what a metal band can be. They have inspired a wave of new artists to combine different genres, especially ones that adopt a cultural flavour from different countries, paving the way for more diverse and experimental music.

Your thoughts and reviews:

☆☆☆☆☆

Bee Gees

Born on the Isle of Man during the late 1940s the Gibb brothers emigrated to Australia in 1958 before returning to the UK where they embarked on a music career that saw them sell over two hundred million records worldwide. While most widely known for their disco hits of the late 1970s, their career had exploded much earlier with hit albums and singles released during the late 1960s.

The brothers Barry, born in 1946, and twins Robin and Maurice, born in 1949, began their career in music entertaining crowds at half-time at their local speedway stadium in Queensland before promoter Bill Goode introduced them to Brisbane radio-presenter Bill Gates (not that one). He came up with the name 'the BGs' after his, Goode's and Barry Gibb's initials.

Frustrated by their lack of success the Brothers Gibb returned to the UK in 1967, shortly after which they released "New York Mining Disaster 1941". With a sound not dissimilar to the Beatles and a record sleeve only displaying the song title, radio DJs assumed it was the Fab Four and put it on heavy rotation. The ruse worked as the single hit Number 12 while the album *Bee Gees 1st* peaked at Number 8.

The group followed this up with the album *Horizontal*, which included their first Number 1 "Massachusetts" and a promotional tour to the US which saw the LAPD on high alert and anticipating the type of reception regularly received by musicians jetting in from the UK at that time.

Similar artists:

Air Supply
Chicago
Earth, Wind and Fire
Diana Ross

The brothers briefly disbanded in 1969 with solo projects yielding various levels of success. After regrouping in 1972 single "Run to Me" returned them to the Top 10 but by 1974 their success had waned once more so they started to craft more dance-oriented, disco songs. This saw both 1975's "Jive Talkin'" and the following year's "You Should Be Dancing" both peak at Number 5.

1977's *Saturday Night Fever* soundtrack proved to be the group's turning point with both the film and music impacting across the world while enhancing disco's mainstream appeal. Their music became synonymous with the genre and their influence extended far beyond the dancefloors.

The album produced three Top 5 singles while the soundtrack broke multiple industry records, selling over forty million copies and becoming the highest-selling album in recording history. If that wasn't enough, in the meantime Barry had also written the title song to *Grease* for Frankie Valli. Unfortunately the glow of the disco ball soon burst, fuelled as much by homophobia and racism as a disdain for the music. The band had however predicted this and their follow-up single "Too Much Heaven" was a deliberate attempt to distance themselves from the genre.

While 1979's *Spirits Having Flown* saw them reach Number 1 around the world, 1981's *Living Eyes* only reached Number 73 in the UK although it did have the distinction of being the first compact disc ever played in public when it was aired on *Tomorrow's World*.

Singled out:

"New York Mining Disaster 1941" – Ahead of their assault on the disco genre this Beatlesesque early hit demonstrates a side of the group rarely considered when thinking of the band.

"More Than a Woman" – Simply sublime. If the person you're with doesn't fit the sentiment of this song then maybe you're with the wrong person.

"Stayin' Alive" – When you think of the Bee Gees you think of "Stayin' Alive". Rather aptly, according to the NHS, you can also use the beat to administer amateur CPR.

With *Saturday Night Fever* becoming Saturday night saturation record sales diminished but while the public may have been sick of the sight of the Bee Gees they weren't sick of the sound. Undeterred the band bypassed this reaction by writing hit songs for other artists, which included Barbra Streisand, Dionne Warwick, Dolly Parton & Kenny Rogers and Diana Ross.

Fast forward to 1987 and the band's rollercoaster was back on an upward trajectory. Album *E.S.P.*, buoyed by Number 1 hit "You Win Again", peaked at Number 5 and sold over two million copies. The following three albums all reached the Top 30 while in 1997 the band were once again riding high with their twenty-first album *Still Waters* reaching Number 2.

On the crest of this wave, the brothers performed a Las Vegas concert entitled *One Night Only*. Due to Barry's health, this was due to be their final live performance but it proved less Las Vegas and more Lazarus, as after a positive audience response Barry decided to continue. The concert subsequently expanded into a world tour that included playing to over fifty-six thousand people at Wembley Stadium.

Album of the week: *Spirits Having Flown*

The Bee Gees' fifteenth album rode high on the success of 1977's *Saturday Night Fever*, reaching Number 1 in the UK and various other countries. It sold over thirty million records worldwide and spawned three Top 20 hit singles, "Love You Inside Out", the Number 1 hit "Tragedy" and the first single off the album "Too Much Heaven", released deliberately as a remedy to the 'disco' tag the band had generated since *Saturday Night Fever*.

The title track was also released at the end of the year to promote the band's greatest hits album and peaked at Number 16.

Brother Maurice was said to have contributed far less to this album although this was due to back pains finally diagnosed in 1980 caused by a bad disk – probably their first bad disc since 1970's *Cucumber Castle* album!

The group released their final album *This Is Where I Came In* in 2001 and saw it reach Number 6. Following Maurice's sudden death in 2003 Barry and Robin retired the group's name but in 2009 Robin announced he and Barry had agreed the Bee Gees would re-form and perform again, however, Robin passed away in May 2012 with the brothers leaving a remarkable musical legacy.

Your thoughts and reviews:

Björk

Björk Guðmundsdóttir, known mononymously as Björk, is renowned for her eclectic style, experimental approach to music and captivating stage presence. She has released eleven studio albums and twenty-two hit singles with record sales ranging from twenty to forty million depending on who you speak to. Noted for her distinct three-octave vocal range her sound draws on electronic, pop, experimental, trip-hop, classical and avant-garde music although she has consistently defied categorisation in a career spanning four decades.

Born in 1965, Björk enrolled at Reykjavík school Barnamúsíkskóli at the age of six where she studied classical piano and flute. After a school recital of Tina Charles's "I Love to Love" her teachers sent a recording to the RÚV radio station, the choice of which came easy as it was Iceland's *only* radio station.

Her debut album *Björk* was recorded when she was just eleven years old but only released in her native Iceland and not considered part of her discography due to her age.

During her teens and early twenties Björk formed and starred in numerous bands, eventually gaining international recognition at the age of twenty-one as lead singer of the Sugarcubes. The album *Life's Too Good*, with signature single "Birthday", was an unexpected success and is credited as the first Icelandic album to hit the mainstream.

Similar artists:

Fiona Apple
Arca
Cocteau Twins
Goldfrapp

During her time with the Sugarcubes Björk contributed vocals to 808 State's 1991 album *ex:el*, which cultivated her interest in house music. Her first international solo hit "Human Behaviour" reached the Top 40 while 1993's *Debut* peaked at Number 3. The album's eclectic sound proved hugely successful and opened up the doors to her collaborating with artists including PJ Harvey, David Arnold, Tricky and Madonna.

Building on the success of *Debut* Björk continued to pursue different sounds in her second album *Post*. Produced in conjunction with Nellee Hooper, Tricky, Graham Massey and Howie B, the album included six hit singles, three of which reached the Top 10 while the album peaked at Number 2.

Paparazzi intrusion and an assassination attempt led Björk to leave London for Spain before recording her next album *Homogenic*. Released in 1997 it is one of Björk's most experimental works, continuing to push musical boundaries and solidify her reputation as an avant-garde artist.

Subsequent albums continued to see Björk experiment with both sound and distribution. Her greatest hits album, released in 2002, was formed of songs chosen by fans while 2004's *Medúlla* was entirely vocal-based, using the skills of a throat singer, beatboxer and choirs. 2011's *Biophilia* included an app album that included workshops for schoolchildren exploring the connection between music and science, which impressed the Reykjavik City Board of Education so much that they added it to the curriculum.

Singled out:

"Jóga" – Fusing lush strings with rocky electronic crunches but more importantly Björk's distinctive and impassioned voice, which barely manages to keep from breaking but manages it does.

"Play Dead" – A track in which the diminutive singer seems to be in combat with the massive orchestra and comes out on top. Throw in the contemporary percussion for an incredible final result.

"Big Time Sensuality" – You can't bottle joy but this track makes you imagine what dogs are feeling when they stick their heads out of car windows.

In addition to her musical career, Björk also starred in the 2000 film *Dancer in the Dark*. After asking her to write the soundtrack, director Lars von Trier also convinced her to play the character of Selma, which resulted in her winning the Best Actress Award at that year's Cannes Film Festival.

Such was Björk's influence on both music and art in general that in 2015 a full-scale retrospective exhibition dedicated to her was held at the Museum of Modern Art. Meanwhile her activism and advocacy for environmental and social causes are also noteworthy. She has been outspoken about climate change and the importance of preserving nature with her latest offering, the 2023 single "Oral", supporting residents of Seyðisfjörður in the campaign against Norwegian-owned fish farming operations.

Album of the week: *Debut*

If we're being pedantic, Björk's actual debut album appeared sixteen years prior to this one when released in her native Iceland in 1993.

While record company One Little Indian predicted the album would sell forty thousand copies, it eventually went on to sell almost five million worldwide.

Five of the eleven tracks on the album were released and charted in the UK, three of which, "Play Dead", "Big Time Sensuality" and "Violently Happy" all reached the Top 20.

Debut was an extensive departure from the rock music of Björk's previous band the Sugarcubes and drew from a variety of styles. The songs didn't fit with the music Björk was performing at the time. On release it therefore flew in the face of the guitar-wielding grunge zeitgeist and the emergence of Britpop.

Heavily influenced by the British dance scene the album is credited as being among the first to bring house music into the mainstream. Björk was also influenced by the tabla-playing Talvin Singh and even David Attenborough, singing lyrics to "Human Behaviour" from the point of view of an animal.

Björk's use of unconventional instruments combined with her mastery of electronic music production has created a sound that is both otherworldly and deeply personal. Meanwhile her fearless experimentation and her willingness to explore unconventional themes have set her apart from other musicians and artists. She has drawn inspiration from a wide range of sources including nature, technology and human emotions, incorporating them into her music in unique ways that have led to her being one step ahead of both critics and supporters alike.

Your thoughts and reviews:

☆ ☆ ☆ ☆ ☆

Blondie

Blondie was synonymous with the new wave scene that typified the 1970s and was the first group from that category to have mainstream success. However, it's often impossible to pin them down to a particular genre as their songs cover a range of styles, which include disco, pop, reggae, rap and rock. They were inducted into the Rock and Roll Hall of Fame in 2006 having sold over forty million records worldwide, with their third album *Parallel Lines* selling twenty million copies alone.

Formed in New York in 1974, Blondie took its name from regular comments hurled at lead singer Debbie Harry from misogynistic truck drivers across the United States. Influences came in the form of pop majesty David Bowie and Iggy Pop who they supported in 1977. They also played in clubs alongside the likes of Patti Smith and at the same time enjoyed the once-in-a-lifetime opportunity of supporting Talking Heads.

Harry met Chris Stein in 1973 when he joined her in a group called the Stilettoes. The band lasted just a year with Harry and Stein walking out of the Stilettoes, or rather tottering, along with bandmate Elda Gentile.

There followed a revolving door of musicians until Blondie became an established six-piece band although as Debbie Harry began to attain a celebrity status the other members were sadly largely ignored by the media (and gladly, misogynistic trucker drivers).

Similar artists:

Joan Jett and the Blackhearts
The Pretenders
Ramones
T. Rex

The band's self-titled debut album initially failed to chart in 1976, which the band blamed on poor publicity and so ended their record deal with Private Stock early. Success did come over in Australia the following year however, when instead of playing the music video to debut single "X-Offender" a TV programme played B-side "In the Flesh", which serendipitously became their first hit.

After buying themselves out of the Private Stock contract Blondie signed with British label Chrysalis. The label re-released the band's debut album alongside their second, *Plastic Letters*. On the back of this *Blondie* peaked at Number 75 while *Plastic Letters*, bolstered by the Top 10 hits "Denis" and "(I'm Always Touched by Your) Presence, Dear" reached the Top 10.

At this time the band were enjoying prolonged success in the UK and Australia while in the US they were still seen as an underground band. *Plastic Letters* had crept into the US Chart at a disappointing Number 72 but this was to change with the release of the band's third album *Parallel Lines*.

The album was preceded by the single "Picture This", which peaked at Number 12 while the album contained a further three hit singles, "Hanging on the Telephone", "Heart of Glass" and "Sunday Girl", the latter two of which reached Number 1. The album hit the Number 1 slot in the UK and finally saw the band enjoy success in the US, peaking at Number 6 while selling over twenty million copies worldwide.

Singled out:

"Rapture" – Blondie cut faultlessly across a number of genres even within the same song, as this record proves as it makes a seamless journey across soul, funk and rap.

"Atomic" – A timeless classic from 1980 with a driving bassline and percussion. When Sleeper recorded this over fifteen years later they didn't change a single thing.

"For Your Eyes Only" – The Bond theme that never was as Sheena Easton played along and performed the film producers' song, whereas Blondie wanted to perform their own.

Blondie were on a roll and their follow-up album *Eat to the Beat* also peaked at Number 1. Single "Dreaming" reached Number 2 while "Atomic" went one better to reach the top spot. Despite the track having everlasting appeal, the band admitted that neither the title nor the lyrics had any real meaning. Meanwhile "Call Me", taken from the *American Gigolo* soundtrack also reached Number 1, as did the first single from 1980's *Autoamerican* album "The Tide is High". This made it three Number 1s in a row and all within the same year.

Autoamerican reached the Top 10, as did 1982's *The Hunter*, after which the group disbanded. They took a fifteen-year hiatus before returning, during which time Debbie Harry pursued a solo career while also caring for bandmate Chris Stein who had a long-term illness. She had already released the Top 10 album *KooKoo* in 1981 following this up with a further three albums between 1986 and 1993.

Album of the week: *Parallel Lines*

You'd be forgiven for thinking that an album produced in six weeks, even though record label Chrysalis gave them six months, was a breeze but far from it. The creation of the album was beset with struggles within the band with lyricist and singer Debbie Harry still composing the words in the seconds before recording them. Meanwhile their producer at the time thought the group were one of the least talented set of musicians he'd ever worked with, completely missing the point of the punk genre altogether.

Despite reservations from the label, the band believed the album would reach a wider audience than the previous album *Plastic Letters*. They were proved right with the album eventually selling over twenty million records worldwide and influencing a plethora of other New York bands.

Of the four singles released, two, "Heart of Glass" and "Sunday Girl", reached Number 1.

Thirty-four years later "One Way or Another" reached the Top 100 in downloads after being covered by One Direction for charity.

On their return in 1999 album *No Exit* reached Number 3. This included the single *Maria*, which saw Debbie Harry as the oldest female singer, at the age of fifty-three, to have a UK Number 1 at that time.

Blondie's last album *Pollinator*, released in 2017, saw them reach the public's consciousness once again, peaking at Number 4 while the band's latest tour took place throughout 2022 while 2023 saw them perform at the 22nd Coachella Valley Music and Arts Festival.

Your thoughts and reviews:

Kate Bush

Kate Bush's appearance on the music scene heralded a number of firsts, which for 1978 seems unfathomable. She was the first British solo female to top the UK Album Chart, first female artist to enter the UK Album Chart at Number 1, first female to have written every track on a million-selling debut album, first female artist to achieve a UK Number 1 with a self-written song and in 2013 becoming the only female artist to have Top 5 albums in five successive decades.

Born in 1958 in Bexleyheath, Kent, it was the musical influence of her family that inspired Kate Bush to teach herself the piano at the age of eleven while also studying the violin. While her family produced a demo tape, which included over fifty of her songs, they failed to find a record label. It wasn't until David Gilmour of Pink Floyd fame got hold of a copy and worked his magic to create a more professional recording did the record industry take note. Bush was duly signed to EMI.

Bush released her debut album *The Kick Inside* when she was nineteen although it featured songs written when she was just thirteen. EMI wanted "James and the Cold Gun" to be her debut single but in an incredibly bold move for a young woman in the male-dominated industry Bush insisted that it should be "Wuthering Heights". She was proved right when the single became the first Number 1 written by a female artist and topped the chart for four weeks. The album itself peaked at Number 3 and has since sold over one million copies.

Similar artists:

Tori Amos
Weyes Blood
Björk
Suzanne Vega

EMI wanted to record a quick follow-up album, again against Bush's wishes, to take advantage of the success of *The Kick Inside* and so *Lionheart* was released the same year. The singer was once more proven right when, although reaching Number 6, the LP remains Bush's least successful album. The subsequent six-week run of concerts however was literally a tour de force and demonstrated Bush's ambition to combine a strong visual stage presence alongside her inimitable singing style. It would be a further twenty-six years before Kate Bush performed live again when she began a twenty-two-night residency at London's Hammersmith Apollo in 2014.

1980s album *Never for Ever* saw Bush evolve her musical style by adopting synthesisers and drum machines, which allowed her to sample and manipulate sounds and expand her sonic range. Three singles hit the Top 20 with "Babooshka" the pick of the bunch, peaking at Number 5. The album entered the chart at Number 1, making her the first female British artist to do so and therefore giving her another 'first' to add to the mantel.

Despite early EMI gaffs, it took four albums before Bush gained artistic independence from record company bosses who by now must have been choking on humble pie. *The Dreaming* was her first record in the production seat while by the time *Hounds of Love* was released in 1985 she had built her own private studio. The album contained four Top 40 singles including the Number 3 hit "Running Up That Hill", which again saw Number 1 success.

Singled out:

"Running Up That Hill" – Eventually becoming a Number 1 hit in 2022, thirty-seven years after its original release, demonstrates the enduring quality of Kate Bush's music.

"Don't Give Up" – A song that shows just how powerful a single track can be. Elton John credited this track with saving his life and it has no doubt done the same for countless others.

"Wuthering Heights" – We don't use the word 'wuthering' enough. As epic as Emily Brontë's 1847 novel, this 1978 hit is just as timeless and sways like the wind across the Yorkshire Moors.

Bush's next two albums, *The Sensual World* and *The Red Shoes*, both reached Number 2, after which she took a twelve-year hiatus. She made a comeback with 2005's *Aerial* with her appeal continuing and seeing the album peak at Number 3. Notable tracks included "Pi" in which Bush sings one hundred and seventeen digits of the mathematical constant while the title track of her final 2011 album *50 Words for Snow* features a list of words to describe that particular form of precipitation. Neither of these were released as a single.

1985 single "Running Up That Hill" received fresh interest in 2022 after appearing in the TV series *Stranger Things*. Now streamable it became Bush's second Number 1 while giving it the backhanded compliment of being the single with the longest period of time taken to get to the top spot. The track also ensured that, at the age of sixty-three, she replaced Cher as the oldest female solo chart-topping artist.

Album of the week: *Hounds of Love*

Of the nine studio albums released by Kate Bush only *Lionheart* fell out of the Top 5 (and only just, peaking at Number 6). Finding a definitive album from the singer's collection is therefore tough.

Having taken two years to complete, the album could've easily been titled *Labour of Love* but eventually sold over one million copies worldwide.

Although CDs had been all the rage since 1982 Bush still utilised the traditional A-side/B-side format of vinyl LPs and tapes, attaching the singles to the A-side while giving over the B-side to a conceptual half about a woman drifting alone in the sea at night.

The fifth track "Cloudbusting" peaked at Number 20 and was later sampled by Utah Saints in their 1992 Top 5 hit "Something Good".

"Running Up That Hill" became a Number 3 hit when originally released before hitting Number 1 in the UK and around the world thirty-seven years later when featured substantially on the soundtrack to the TV series *Stranger Things*, at the behest of actress Wynona Ryder.

Bush's eclectic musical style, unconventional lyrics, live performances and literary themes have catapulted her into the minds and imaginations of devoted followers for over forty years while influencing a diverse range of other artists. Her career has yielded twenty-five Top 40 singles while all but one of her ten studio albums have reached the Top 5.

Your thoughts and reviews:

☆ ☆ ☆ ☆ ☆

Johnny Cash

Johnny Cash is one of the most prolific and best-selling music artists of all time, recording over one and a half thousand songs across ninety-six albums. He has sold more than ninety million records in a career spanning over forty-five years. Known for his deep, resonant voice, rebellious spirit, and captivating storytelling, his music embraced country, rock and roll, blues and gospel, with most containing themes of sorrow and redemption. His family's economic and personal struggles during the Great Depression gave him a lifelong sympathy for the poor and working class and inspired many of his songs that appealed to the very same people.

Johnny Cash was born in 1932 to poor cotton farmers and started working on the farm at the age of five, singing with the family as they worked. His mother bought him a guitar at the age of ten and he began playing and writing songs at the age of twelve.

Tragedy struck in 1944 when Johnny's older brother Jack was killed in an accident at work, which further encouraged Johnny to sing about the plight of America's blue-collar workers. The subjects of his songs also include empathy with those in prison and indigenous people of the US, with his 1964 album *Bitter Tears: Ballads of the American Indian* devoted to songs addressing the plight of Native Americans. While at odds with the usual themes of country music, which often focus on the plight of the cowboys, the record reached the US Top 50 and Number 2 on the US Country Chart.

Similar artists:

- Merle Haggard
- The Highwaymen
- Willie Nelson
- Hank Williams

Even before his music career began Johnny Cash was to have an exciting and eventful life. In 1950 he enlisted in the US Air Force and was assigned to the 12th Radio Squadron. Tasked with intercepting Soviet Army transmissions he is said to have been the first American to hear of the death of Joseph Stalin, second leader of the Soviet Union. This claim is backed up by his daughter who said he recounted the story often, although my Grandad used to tell us he drove through Checkpoint Charlie in a tank so who knows?

In 1954 Cash approached Sam Phillips at Sun Records with a collection of mostly gospel songs. After initial rejection with Phillips saying that he no longer produced gospel records Cash returned and won over the producer with a more rockabilly sound.

A year later Cash made his first recordings for Sun Records and in 1956 he found himself in exalted company, joining fellow artists including Elvis Presley, Jerry Lee Lewis and Carl Perkins in an opportune jam session. The recording was found in 1969 when Shelby Singleton bought the record label with the album subsequently released across Europe in 1981 as *Million Dollar Quartet*. More material was later unearthed resulting in *The Complete Million Dollar Session*, released in 1987 and repackaged and released as *Elvis Presley: The Million Dollar Quartet* across the US in 1990. Sixteen years later a fiftieth anniversary edition was published while the release of *The Million Dollar Quartet Flogs a Dead Horse* is yet to be confirmed.

Singled out:

"Ring Of Fire" – Unmistakably Johnny Cash, this crossover hit reached Number 1 on the US Country Charts while also featuring heavily in the pop charts.

"A Boy Named Sue" – Recorded live at San Quentin prison, this track captures the humorous side of country music, perfectly wrapping up a full story in a self-contained 3:42 single.

"Hurt" – Not many people write their own epitaph but in covering this Nine Inch Nails track Cash offered an unguarded apology while showing his unequivocal ability to cover a wide range of artists.

Cash left Sun Records in 1958 to sign a contract with Columbia but left behind sufficient recordings that were still being released as late as 1964. The late 1950s also saw what was one of the most unique elements of his illustrious career as he performed at various prisons across the US, including to what you could say was a captive audience at San Quentin State Prison in 1958. These performances would later result in two successful live albums, *At Folsom Prison* in 1968 and *At San Quentin* in 1969, in a year when his six-and-a-half million album sales eclipsed even that of the Beatles. "A Boy Named Sue" recorded live at San Quenton peaked at Number 4 in the UK.

By the mid-1970s Cash's popularity began to decline and saw him revert to making TV adverts. His career was rejuvenated in the 1990s however after meeting record producer Rick Rubin and seeing his traditional country music cross over into the mainstream.

In 1994 Cash released *American Recordings*, accompanied only by his Martin Dreadnought guitar. The album featured covers of artists ranging from Tom Waits to Leonard Cohen while his later recordings in the *American I-VI* series would include covers of bands as diverse as Soundgarden, Nine Inch Nails and Depeche Mode.

Album of the week: *Hello, I'm Johnny Cash*

Cramming twelve songs into just over thirty-seven minutes, Johnny Cash's thirty-third album chugs along on a joyously relentless mix of rolling percussion and bouncing bass guitar. It's no surprise that the eleventh track "I've Got a Thing About Trains" is a love letter to this ailing form of transport.

The LP was Cash's first UK Top 10 album, peaking at Number 6 just as it did on the other side of the pond.

While the singles failed to chart in the UK, "If I Were a Carpenter", penned by American folk and blues musician Tim Hardin, earned Cash, along with his wife, a Grammy Award in 1969. They also won the Best Country Performance by a Duo or Group with Vocal.

June Carter Cash, Johnny's second wife, passed away in May 2003 aged 73. Johnny continued to work at her behest and went on to complete sixty songs in the last four months of his life. He died of complications from diabetes aged seventy-one. Of the four studio albums released posthumously, three of them reached the Top 10 in the UK with the final album *Out Among the Stars* peaking at Number 4.

Your thoughts and reviews:

☆ ☆ ☆ ☆ ☆

Tracy Chapman

Tracy Chapman's passionate, soulful voice and thought-provoking lyrics have left an indelible mark on the music industry since she took to a stage in 1988. Beyond her definitive soulful sound, her music is infused with a deep sense of social consciousness and a commitment to addressing issues such as social justice, poverty, inequality, racism and political unrest. Tender yet incredibly determined her music continues to have the ability to urge listeners to confront these challenges head-on.

Tracy Chapman was born in Cleveland, Ohio, in 1964. Her mother, who would become a professional American footballer, bought her a ukelele at the age of three and by the age of eight she was playing guitar and writing her own songs. It was here that Chapman experienced the race-related bullying that would later play out in the more political elements of her music.

Chapman was sponsored to attend high school away from her home community and therefore ended up studying over five hundred miles from her native Cleveland in Connecticut. The move proved serendipitous however as during her studies at nearby Tufts University in Boston she would hone her craft by busking in the local neighbourhood while also meeting fellow student Brian Koppelman. Brian's father Charles was a musician and music producer who Brian introduced Chapman to and who helped her sign a contract with Elektra Records in 1987.

Similar artists:

Macy Gray
Nora Jones
Joni Mitchell
Nina Simone

In 1988 Chapman released her eponymous debut album and within two weeks of its release it had sold one million copies, eventually going on to sell over twenty million worldwide. The album contained three of Chapman's most recognisable singles including "Talkin' 'bout a Revolution", "Baby Can I Hold You" and the Number 4 hit single "Fast Car". It was the latter hit which catapulted Chapman to international recognition after she performed the song at the Nelson Mandela 70th Birthday Tribute concert at Wembley Stadium in June that year.

The singer was initially booked to perform a slot in the afternoon but again the music gods of serendipity shone Chapman's way. Her music career was signed, sealed and delivered after repeating her set as a last-minute stand-in for Stevie Wonder whose backing track was lost. Wonder refused to perform and Chapman retook her place onstage in front of a capacity crowd, broadcast in sixty-seven countries to a worldwide audience of six hundred million people. Chapman was just twenty-five years old and with nothing but a two-month-old album and an acoustic guitar she became an instant hit.

Chapman followed up her debut album a year later with the self-produced *Crossroads*. While the lead track of the same name fared less well than previous singles, peaking at Number 61, the album hit Number 1 in the UK and the Top 10 around the world, selling over one million copies in the US and over three hundred thousand in the UK.

Singled out:

"Talking 'bout a Revolution" – A quiet call to arms that's almost lost among the slight guitar and Chapman's wistful voice. It's a song to take the gates while the aggressors fail to hear.

"Fast Car" – I wish I'd had the confidence at twenty-five to sing in front of a worldwide TV audience of six hundred million people but I guess if I'd written this song then I'd have that confidence.

"Baby Can I Hold You" – Teetering on the brittle edge of sincere ballad and rom-com finale mush, this thankfully just falls on the right side. Boyzone's 1997 version fell on the other.

The singer went on to release six further albums. 1992's *Matters of the Heart* peaked at Number 19 while the fourth album *New Beginning* sold five million copies in the US although failed to chart in the UK. Chapman's final four studio albums released between 2000 and 2008 achieved varying degrees of success, meanwhile a compilation album *Collection* released in 2001 reached Number 3.

Further success was to come in 2023 when she became the first black woman to achieve a Number 1 with a solo composition in the US Country Chart after Luke Combs' version of "Fast Car" hit the top spot.

The impact of Tracy Chapman's career however extends beyond music and has served as a soundtrack for social movements, inspiring individuals to engage in activism and advocate for justice. Meanwhile her contributions to humanitarian causes and her work to address environmental issues have further amplified her influence.

Album of the week: *Tracy Chapman*

Tracy Chapman's eponymous album was an instant success, selling over one million copies in its first two weeks alone and eventually over twenty million worldwide.

It took incredible faith to produce, not least of all from the artist herself who didn't believe her music had much commercial appeal. This was epitomised when Chapman initially didn't take an acquaintance at university seriously when he told her that his father was a producer in the music industry.

Buoyed by the single "Fast Car", which peaked at Number 4, Chapman's music was seen as an antidote to the synthetic saccharine pop music of the time.

However, the stripped-back simplistic nature of the music just needed an audience to tune into the simple sincerity of the album.

When Chapman appeared at the Nelson Mandela 70th Birthday Tribute concert in June 1988, the audience was assured and her career exploded.

As well as the Nelson Mandela Birthday Tribute Tracy Chapman also featured on the worldwide Amnesty International Human Rights Now! tour that same year and ten years later performed at the 50th anniversary of Amnesty International in Paris. In 1997 she sang at the inaugural Lilith Fair, founded by Canadian singer-songwriter Sarah McLachlan in response to the lack of opportunities for female musicians in the industry. Later, in 2004, Chapman rode in the AIDS/LifeCycle event and in 2008 was commissioned by the American Conservatory Theater to compose music for a play about South African apartheid.

Your thoughts and reviews:

Chic

Chic was formed in 1972 by Nile Rodgers and Bernard Edwards. With their distinctive sound characterised by infectious guitar riffs and tight basslines, they became one of the powerhouses of disco. With their blend of disco, funk and R&B they became synonymous with danceable grooves and stylish fashion with signature afros, sharp suits and extravagant accessories making them style icons of the era. In addition to their own success Rodgers and Edwards were prolific producers and songwriters, collaborating with an impressive roster of artists throughout a glistening career.

Nile Rodgers and Bernard Edwards met in 1970 as session musicians working in New York with their first taste of fame coming as part of the imaginatively named band New York City and their 1973 hit "I'm Doing Fine Now".

After watching English rock band Roxy Music in concert Rodgers was inspired to form a group that would be as much about the image as about the music, taking further inspiration from US rockers Kiss and going on to create one of the most visually striking groups of the era.

Along with other members of the band, which included Luther Vandross at one point, before he went solo, the pair added Norma Jean Wright on vocals in 1977 and produced their eponymous debut album that same year. While this didn't chart in the UK, singles "Dance, Dance, Dance (Yowsah, Yowsah, Yowsah)" and "Everybody Dance" both made the Top 10.

Similar artists:

- KC & the Sunshine Band
- Tom McGuire & the Brassholes
- Sister Sledge
- Tavares

In 1978 Norma Jean left to work on solo projects, paving the way for Alfa Anderson to join. Anderson had sung backing vocals on album *Chic* and was joined that year by Luci Martin with Edwards and Rodgers convinced that they needed two female vocalists to recreate the band's studio sound when performing live.

Their follow-up to *Chic*, *C'est Chic* (or titled *Très Chic* when released across Europe) again spawned two Top 10 singles in "I Want Your Love" and "Le Freak" and sold over one million copies. The unmistakable 'Freak out!' lyric of the latter was originally penned as an expletive to a doorman who had barred their entry to Studio 54 but instead of entering the club they went home and wrote the track that ended up selling over seven million copies.

The third album *Risqué*, released in 1979, did not fare as well as their previous album but it did feature one of the most influential songs of the era. "Good Times" was a Number 5 hit, with a distinctive bassline that has since been the basis of Grandmaster Flash's "Adventures on the Wheels of Steel" and the Sugarhill Gang's "Rapper's Delight", heavily influencing the future sound of hip-hop. It has also been sampled by Queen, Blondie and Daft Punk.

After the backlash against disco music at the end of the 1970s the band struggled for commercial success with their four albums released between 1980 and 1983 failing to chart in the UK. This included the 1982 album *Tongue in Chic*, which surely deserves a Top 10 position on name alone.

Singled out:

- "Dance, Dance, Dance (Yowsah, Yowsah, Yowsah)" – The tight bassline of Bernard Edwards and funky strum of Nile Rogers epitomised the sound of Chic right from the outset.

- "I Want Your Love" – Clanging chimes add an almost melancholic edge to this disco hit, which epitomises the highs and lows of a love that this track describes.

- "Good Times" – With a bassline used by Grandmaster Flash, the Sugarhill Gang, Queen, Blondie and Daft Punk, this has been recycled more times than your milk bottles.

As well as writing music for Chic, Edwards and Rodgers have also composed, arranged, performed and produced many records for a range of artists throughout their career. This was most notable with Sister Sledge but they also worked with Diana Ross, Carly Simon and Debbie Harry. They would later work with artists as eclectic as David Bowie, Madonna, the Thompson Twins, Duran Duran and Daft Punk.

The group disbanded in 1983 but after positive response to them playing Chic songs at a party in 1989 Rodgers and Edwards organised a reunion of the old band. They recorded new material including the 1992 album *Chic-ism*, following this up with a world tour. During 1996 Rodgers' production skills were honoured and he and Edwards embarked on a series of performances again with a range of artists notable for their diversity, from Sister Sledge and Steve Winwood to Simon Le Bon and Slash.

Album of the week: *C'est Chic*

Bizarrely for a band as ubiquitous as Chic this, their second album, is only one of three of their studio LPs to have reached the UK charts, peaking at Number 2 on its release in 1978.

Buoyed by Top 10 singles "I Want Your Love" and their signature tune "Le Freak", which has since sold over seven million copies, the album sold over one million copies in the US and over one hundred thousand in the UK.

The European version differed in both track listing and name, adding their previous two hits "Dance, Dance, Dance (Yowsah, Yowsah, Yowsah)" and "Everybody Dance" to the originally eight-track listing while what was originally *C'est Chic*, translated as 'It's Chic' was also changed to *Très Chic* or 'Very Chic'. The cover also differed, with *Très Chic* featuring a woman wrapped seductively around a neon light whereas the US version features the band relaxing in what looks like a showhome. This may have been down to its risqué nature although could just as easily be due to health and safety concerns over copycats resulting in severe burns.

Bernard Edwards died of pneumonia in 1996 after which Chic continued to tour with new musicians, releasing three compilations and one live album throughout the following decade.

In 2015 Nile Rodgers signed a new record deal and released the first new Chic album in more than two decades, *It's About Time*, which was only their second studio album to reach the Top 10.

Decades after they formed the legacy of Chic lives on, not only through their own discography but also through the countless artists they inspired and influenced. Their music remains a testament to the power of rhythm, groove and the universal desire to dance.

Your thoughts and reviews:

Norman Cook

Norman Cook has secured an everlasting mark on the music industry since he joined the Housemartins as a bassist in 1985. He went on to become one of the most recognised DJs and record producers in the world, helping popularise the big beat genre and leading the emergence of the Superstar DJs at the beginning of the 1990s. His success has come with a variety of monikers and bands across multiple genres and it's this dedication which has led him to become the World Record holder for having the most Top 40 hits under different names.

Changing names came easily for Norman Cook, which is no surprise when given the name Quentin at birth. His parents did have some redeeming factors however with Cook Senior earning himself an MBE for bringing bottle banks to the UK.

Born in Bromley, Kent but raised in Reigate in Surrey, Cook Junior moved to Brighton to study at the local polytechnic where he laid the basis for the city's thriving hip-hop scene. In 1985 he was asked to join the Housemartins by Paul Heaton who he'd previously had a brief flirtation with in a band called the Stomping Pondfrogs. The Housemartins achieved six Top 20 hits during the pinnacle of their success including "Caravan of Love" and "Happy Hour". It was a good place to be but when the band split in 1988 Heaton went on to form the Beautiful South while Cook moved back to Brighton to pursue his interest in dance music.

Similar artists:

Bentley Rhythm Ace
Krafty Kuts
Lo Fidelity Allstars
Mint Royale

It was back in Brighton that in 1989 Cook formed a loose confederation of studio musicians, along with a graffiti artist, called Beats International. Their debut single "Dub Be Good to Me" was a Number 1 hit but this proved to be a disaster with the group using unauthorised samples and lyrics taken from the S.O.S. Band's 1983 hit "Just Be Good to Me". In hindsight maybe the similarity in song titles was a giveaway but either way, the resulting court case led to Cook having to pay back twice the royalties made on the record, which resulted in bankruptcy.

Undeterred Cook came back to have success by forming Freak Power in 1993. Single "Turn On, Tune In, Cop Out" initially reached Number 29 but after being used to advertise Levi's jeans it re-entered the charts two years later and peaked at Number 3.

Cook's next venture was to form the duo Pizzaman with John Reid and once again he possessed the right ingredients for success. While their one album *Pizzamania* didn't end up topping the charts it did include three UK Top 40 singles, "Trippin' on Sunshine", "Sex on the Streets" and "Happiness".

In 1996 Cook adopted the most famous of his monikers, Fatboy Slim, with which he was to become a musical icon. Armed with big beats, catchy hooks, energetic live performances and memorable music videos (one of which included the loveably eccentric Christopher Walken) he would become one of the most recognisable and influential faces in the music industry.

Singled out:

"Dub Be Good to Me" – A jam-hot mix of deep, deep bassline and beautiful female vocals created a track so sublime you'd be happy to be bankrupted by it, which is a good job as it did.

"Eat, Sleep, Rave, Repeat" – A song title that spawned a thousand memes a thousand T-shirt slogans, and maybe a thousand car bumper stickers if we still indulged in car bumper stickers.

"Right Here, Right Now" – Capturing the zeitgeist of the Superstar DJ the big beat percussion and iconic sample gave no illusions that the place to be was indeed, right here and right now.

The project was a slow-burner with debut album *Better Living Through Chemistry* achieving a modest Number 69 in 1996 whereas follow-up *You've Come a Long Way, Baby*, released in 1998, hit Number 1 and sold over five million copies worldwide. The album featured four Top 10 singles including "Right Here, Right Now", which peaked at Number 2 and "Praise You", which was Cook's first solo Number 1.

The success came at a time when DJs were becoming as famous as the artists and bands whose records they were playing, which Cook cemented with a string of high-profile concerts throughout the early 2000s. This included playing to an estimated quarter of a million people at a free show in his adopted Brighton in 2002 and playing the Friday night headline slot on the Other Stage at Glastonbury in 2005.

Album of the week: *You've Come a Long Way, Baby* [E]

Norman Cook's second studio album under the moniker of Fatboy Slim took him from his home studio in Brighton to global fame.

Four tracks from the sample-heavy album, "The Rockafeller Skank", "Gangster Trippin", "Praise You" and "Right Here, Right Now", all supported by incredible MTV-friendly videos, reached the Top 10 while the album went on to sell over five million copies worldwide, bringing the big beat genre to the masses.

Predicting something massive, Cook pushed the boundaries to what was accepted as good taste at the time. The album name comes from a slogan for Virginia Slims cigarettes, the cover features an obese young contestant from the 1983 Fat People's Festival in the US and the third track

"F****** in Heaven" pulls no punches either.

Distributors in the US weren't impressed and changed the cover to one showing a library of records while altering the offensive track title to simply "In Heaven". (You may wish to do the same depending on the age of your kids, while skipping the track entirely if they're very young.)

Cook released a greatest hits collection, *Why Try Harder*, in 2006, consisting of his own tracks as well as songs remixed for other bands. These included Cornershop's "Brimful of Asha" and Groove Armada's "I See You Baby". Cook also produced Rizzle Kicks' "Mama Do the Hump", which peaked at Number 2 in 2011 and in 2013 returned to the upper echelons of the charts himself with "Eat, Sleep, Rave, Repeat", which peaked at Number 3.

He has continued to dabble in the music industry under the Fatboy Slim moniker with a string of non-charting releases since 2017 while appearing at the Glastonbury Festival in 2023.

Your thoughts and reviews:

Daft Punk

Daft Punk emerged at the time of a zenith of French house music, using innovative sampling, robotic vocals and a blend of disco, funk, house, electronic and dance that had established artists queuing up to mimic their distinctive sound. They have been widely credited as bringing electronic dance music to the masses, especially so in the US, with some journalists likening them to how the Beatles and others had brought British rock and roll to the American mainstream in the mid-1960s.

Prior to Daft Punk Guy-Manuel de Homem-Christo and Thomas Bangalter had formed a band with schoolmate Laurent Brancowitz called Darlin'. Journalist Dave Jennings wasn't impressed and dubbed their music 'a daft punky thrash' and the name stuck for the pair's new venture.

Homem-Christo was born in Neuilly-sur-Seine in 1974, with his earliest musical forays performed on a toy guitar and keyboard given to him before he was ten. Bangalter, born in Paris a year later, began playing the piano at the age of six, taking lessons from a staff member of the Opéra de Paris. The pair met in 1987 at the Lycée Carnot secondary school in the French capital.

The pair's debut single "The New Wave" was given a limited release and failed to chart. The second single "Da Funk" however, released in 1995, reached Number 7. After being touted by a number of record labels they signed with Virgin, who promised the pair more creative control of their music.

Similar artists:

The Chemical Brothers
deadmau5
MGMT
Justice

Following the release of "Da Funk" Daft Punk released their debut album *Homework* in 1997 to similar success, seeing it peak at Number 8. The second single from the album "Around the World" carried on from where "Da Funk" left off and hit the Top 20 not so much around the world but certainly across Europe. Their style was immediately copied by other artists, most notably Madonna who was soon collaborating with French electronic dance producer Mirwais Ahmadzaï to add a sprinkling of their sound to four of her Madjesty's studio albums between 2000 and 2019.

The band's second album *Discovery* took four years to produce and yielded similar success. With a string of hit singles including "Digital Love", "Harder, Better, Faster, Stronger" and Number 2 hit "One More Time" the album peaked at Number 2 and sold over two million records across Europe alone.

It was between the release of these two albums that the duo started appearing in their distinctive robot costumes, using helmets, outfits and gloves to disguise their identities while making few media appearances. Before this Homem-Christo and Bangalter had worn Halloween masks or bags for promotional appearances in the hope that their music would do the talking. The costumes also allowed the pair to control their image and retain their anonymity, protecting their personal lives while building up an element of mystique. At a cost of $65,000 the helmets, designed by Tony Gardner who was inspired by the sci-fi classic *The Day the Earth Stood Still,* were certainly no gimmick.

Singled out:

- "Around the World" – Such was the band's influence that 1997 saw partygoers shambolically mimic the robotic dance featured in the music video all across the continent.

- "One More Time" – A perfect demonstration of Daft Punk's pioneering technique of drenching music in treble before raising the bass to a devastating dancefloor effect.

- "Digital Love" – This delight from the *Discovery* album fills you with all the joyful childlike naivety of the Buggles' "Video Killed the Radio Star".

The third album *Human After All* took just six weeks to write and produce but showed Daft Punk's vulnerability. The LP received mixed reviews when released in 2005 but still managed to claw its way into the UK's Top 10. The subsequent forty-eight-date world tour however, which spanned 2006 and 2007, fared better and has been credited for bringing dance music to a wider audience.

Following the tour the band started working on what would become the soundtrack to the 2010 film *Tron: Legacy*. The record was produced over two years and resulted in an eighty-five-piece orchestra recreating the music written by the pair.

In 2013 Daft Punk released their final album *Random Access Memories*. Preceded by the global smash "Get Lucky", recorded with Pharrell Williams and Nile Rodgers, the band secured the Number 1 spot across the world. High demand provided further collaborations with the pair adding Kanye West, Jay-Z and the Weeknd to their musical CV.

Album of the week: *Random Access Memories*

Daft Punk's fourth and final album took four years to produce, during which time they released the soundtrack to *Tron: Legacy*.

The album was launched at the annual Wee Waa show based in the small rural Australian town of Wee Waa in 2013, which saw the town's population double when the album was live-streamed in front of a crowd of over four thousand.

The record saw the band move away from their well-established use of samples and loops as they hoped to bring a more human element to music, although they still stood steadfast to the vocoder. Instead they reverted to live instruments and employed an array of collaborators including disco pioneer Giorgio Moroder, Nile Rodgers and Pharrell Williams.

The album topped the charts across the globe, eventually selling over three million records worldwide.

Daft Punk released a video on 22 February 2021 featuring a scene from their 2006 film *Electroma* in which one robot explodes and the other walks away, along with a title which read '1993–2021'. Later that day their publicist confirmed that the duo had split with the news leading to a surge in Daft Punk sales that saw digital album purchases rising by almost three thousand percent.

Your thoughts and reviews:

☆ ☆ ☆ ☆ ☆

Depeche Mode

With their innovative blend of electronic beats, soulful vocals and thought-provoking lyrics, Depeche Mode established themselves as one of the most influential bands in music. Over forty years their sound continually evolved to incorporate industrial and alternative rock into their synthpop foundation. They have seen fifty-four hit singles, seventeen Top 10 albums and sold more than one hundred million records, playing live to more than thirty million fans worldwide.

Depeche Mode's original line-up of Vince Clarke, Martin Gore and Andrew Fletcher formed in Basildon, Essex, in 1980. With the advent of affordable synthesizers and the popularity of electronic music, they followed a synth-pop direction but anchored to keyboards and without a drummer the band needed a strong visual front. They found this in Dave Gahan while performing at a scout hut jam session.

The band approached record labels directly with a ruse their demo tape was their only copy, forcing them to play it there and then. However, it was playing live at the Bridge House in Canning Town that Daniel Miller of Mute Records was convinced that Depeche Mode was worth signing. The band's subsequent success put money into the coffers of Miller's Mute Records and enabled him to continue to invest in innovative bands thus paving the way for artists including Goldfrapp, Inspiral Carpets, Moby, Nick Cave and the Bad Seeds and the Prodigy.

Similar artists:

The Cure
Echo & the Bunnymen
New Order
Tears For Fears

Debut single "Dreaming of Me", released in 1981, charted at Number 57 while follow-up "New Life" peaked at Number 11. This resulted in the band's first appearance on *Top of the Pops*, which they travelled to, along with their equipment, by train. The third single "Just Can't Get Enough" became the band's first Top 10 hit and has since been a stalwart of nightclubs as well as being adopted by supporters of multiple sports teams around the world.

Despite their early success Vince Clarke left the band at the end of the year, going on to have success with Yazoo and Erasure. Martin Gore had written a couple of album fillers so stepped forward as the band's songwriter with the resulting *A Broken Frame* peaking at Number 8 and yielding three Top 20 singles, which included the Number 6 hit "See You". Following the album's release Depeche Mode announced Alan Wilder as the fourth member. Wilder had, in fact, been working on the production of *A Broken Frame*, but with the group wanting to keep this quiet to prove they could continue without Clarke.

The third album *Construction Time Again* saw a shift in the group's sound with the introduction of the Synclavier and the E-mu Emulator sampler, presumably without the hand of Rod Hull. The eclectic, industrial-influenced sound resulted in 1984's "People Are People", which saw the band's first success in the US. The single was also used as the theme to West German TV's coverage of the 1984 Olympics and it became an LGBTQ+ anthem, regularly played at gay clubs and gay pride festivals.

Singled out:

"Photographic" – With driving electronics and lyrics that are as unintelligible as the instruction manual for a Commodore 64, this track is the epitome of early 1980s music.

"Personal Jesus" – Like Chablis, the incessant rock-stomp funky bassline and crisp vocals create a mouthwatering accompaniment to any social occasion.

"Walking In My Shoes" – Layers upon layers of sound slowly combine and build up to something quite incredible, like that once-in-a-lifetime lasagna you tasted at that authentic Italian restaurant.

Despite their first six albums all reaching the UK Top 10 Depeche Mode were still considered largely unfavourably in the British music press. The band were unfazed though and even included negative reviews on the sleeve notes of their 1985 singles compilation. Meanwhile in the US the band's following was growing, where fans unencumbered by their earlier appearances in "Smash Hits" and on *Noel Edmonds Multi-Coloured Swap Shop* and *Jimm'll Fix It* saw them as an alternative new-wave band rather than a pop outfit.

In 1986 the band began collaborating with renowned photographer Anton Corbijn who would go on to shape much of their aesthetics including producing videos and directing the band's live shows. This new look was more attuned to the themes that the band had adopted since Gore took up writing duties with songs such as "Blasphemous Rumours" and "Black Celebration" giving them a darker edge.

Two years later global success was growing and saw them conclude their *Music for the Masses* world tour in front of over sixty thousand people at the Pasadena Rose Bowl. 1990's *Violator* created further worldwide appeal while 1993's *Songs of Faith and Devotion* saw the band become only the sixth British act to debut at Number 1 in both the UK and the US.

Album of the week: *Violator*

Concluding 1988's *Music for the Masses* world tour to over sixty thousand people at the Pasadena Rose Bowl hinted at a bright future for Depeche Mode but it was the release of their seventh studio album that saw their global appeal explode.

The single "Personal Jesus" preceded the album in 1989 and has since been covered by artists as diverse as Johnny Cash and Marlyn Manson. Radio-friendly "Enjoy the Silence" became a Top 10 hit on both sides of the Atlantic while later singles "Policy of Truth" and

"World in My Eyes" ensured all four singles on the album hit the Top 20. The album reached Number 2 in the UK and Number 7 in the US, staying in the charts for seventy-four weeks and selling over seven and a half million records.

While the band enjoyed unprecedented success, as individuals they were imploding. Wilder left the band while the three remaining members had their own personal issues resulting in Fletcher leaving their world tour halfway through and Gahan being declared clinically dead for two minutes after a drug overdose.

The band rallied and returned in 1997 with their second Number 1 album *Ultra*. Success continued with six further albums and tours including their *Playing the Angel* world tour watched by almost three million people across thirty-one countries.

In 2022 Andy Fletcher passed away after suffering an aortic dissection. Gahan and Gore continued with their fifteenth studio album *Memento Mori* peaking at Number 2 the following year, accompanied by another world tour throughout 2023 and 2024.

Your thoughts and reviews:

Delia Derbyshire

Referred to as the unsung heroine of British electronic music Delia Derbyshire's work at the BBC Radiophonic Workshop during the 1960s made her an impactful yet little-known figure in electronic music and sound design. She possessed a unique and innovative approach to music, blending traditional composition techniques with cutting-edge technology to create groundbreaking sounds. She left an indelible mark on the world of music and audio production with contemporary artists including Aphex Twin, the Chemical Brothers and Orbital all citing her influence.

Delia Derbyshire was born in Warwickshire in 1937 and developed a love of music after her parents bought her a piano at the age of eight. She was accepted at both Oxford and Cambridge Universities to study maths at a time when only one in ten students were female.

It was at Cambridge that she developed a fascination with sound and its manipulation, switching to study music after the first year and eventually emerging with a BA in mathematics and music.

Derbyshire joined the BBC in 1960 as a trainee assistant studio manager where she heard about the organisation's sound effects department. She applied to work at the grandly entitled Radiophonic Workshop much to the bewilderment of organisation heads who usually had to pressgang people to work in the division.

Similar artists:

Aphex Twin
Brian Hodgson
Éliane Radigue
Laurie Spiegel

At the workshop Derbyshire used basic equipment such as tape recorders, oscillators and filters to create her compositions, meticulously manipulating, splicing together and layering natural and electronic sounds to construct her complex and innovative recordings. The result was a collection of experimental and avant-garde compositions that pushed the boundaries of what was considered music at the time.

One of her first and most widely known compositions came in 1963 when she recreated Ron Grainer's theme for *Doctor Who*. The theme was one of the first created and produced entirely electronically, which Derbyshire created using her usual process of painstakingly cutting, splicing and physically manipulating the tape. While Grainer chivalrously attempted to credit Derbyshire as co-composer however, the BBC bureaucracy preferred members of the workshop to remain anonymous.

In 1966 Derbyshire teamed up with a colleague at the Radiographic Workshop, Brian Hodgson, and founder of Electronic Music Studios, Peter Zinovieff, to set up an organisation to promote the use of electronic music. Named Unit Delta Plus this unfortunately disbanded a year later.

At this time Derbyshire had also recorded a track with Anthony Newley, who'd released a dozen Top 40 hits between 1959 and 1962. Newley moved to the US shortly after though and therefore track "Moogies Bloogies" left us bluegie rather than moogie.

Singled out:

"Theme From Dr Who" – A Kraftwerkesque collision of an incessant bassline with soaring electronic melody, created seven years before Kraftwerk came along.

"Firebird" – Like entering the wrong house party but on the way out you encounter so many fun and interesting people that it takes you all night to leave.

"Theme From The Tomorrow People" – A blend of established TV theme electronic squiggles and giggles but with an added 1970s funkiness that hinted at the future while anchoring it to the age.

At the end of the decade Derbyshire, once again accompanied by Hodgson, teamed up with electronic musician David Vorhaus. The trio set up the Kaleidophon Studio to produce electronic music for London theatre productions. On the back of this project the group formed a band White Noise with the trio releasing one album, 1969's *An Electric Storm*. Although initially unsuccessful the album has since been considered hugely influential in the development of electronic music.

Derbyshire continued to contribute to TV themes and in the 1970s worked on other futuristic programmes. These included *The Tomorrow People* and *Timeslip*, a British children's science fiction television series that only ran for one series between 1970 and 1971.

She left the BBC in 1973 and continued to work independently, collaborating with various artists and musicians while still exploring the potential of synthesizers and computer-generated music. Always at the forefront of technological advancements in the field, she contributed to the soundtrack to *The Legend of Hell House* in 1973 and only stopped producing music in 1975.

Album of the week: *An Electric Storm*

With no solo albums to speak of Delia Derbyshire did join fellow sound technician Brian Hodgson and David Vorhaus, a classical bass player with a background in physics and electronic engineering, to create the band White Noise.

The group's only album, 1969's *An Electric Storm*, started with the intention of only creating a single but grew to a full, thirty-five-minute album at the request of Chris Blackwell of Island Records.

For further indulgence you can join the Delia Derbyshire Appreciation Society. Run by enthusiasts Garry Hughes and Harvey Jones the pair advertise a 'mutual respect for Delia (whom they presume to be on first-name terms with), Eno, Tomita (on surname-terms only), Kraftwerk and a roomful of iconic and mostly working synthesizers'.

Despite her immense talent and groundbreaking contributions to music, Delia Derbyshire faced significant challenges as a woman in a predominantly male-dominated industry. Her work at the BBC Radiophonic Workshop was often underappreciated and overshadowed by her male colleagues. Nevertheless, she persisted and continued to experiment with new techniques and technologies, pushing the boundaries of electronic music further.

After her death in 2001, almost three hundred reel-to-reel tapes and a box of a thousand papers were found in her attic while in recent years there has been a resurgence of interest in her work with documentaries, books and retrospectives dedicated to celebrating her legacy.

Your thoughts and reviews:

The Doors

The Doors stand out as pioneers of psychedelic rock, blending poetic lyrics with mesmerising melodies and leading the surge of iconic bands that emerged during this transformative era of cultural upheaval, political activism and a revolution in music. The band not only opened musical doors but also transcended boundaries with their impact on the cultural landscape of the 1960s and the subsequent evolution of rock music continued long since their end. They would leave an indelible imprint on the soul of rock and roll, instilling the notion that artists could deliver their music without compromise.

The basis of the Doors, or architrave if you like, came on Venice Beach, Los Angeles, in 1965. It was here that alumni of the UCLA School of Theater, Film and Television Ray Manzarek and Jim Morrison crossed paths on a sandy summer stroll.

As with many great bands the meeting of musician (Manzarek) and lyricist (Morrison) spawned a monster of a combination. Manzarek was already in a group with his two brothers with the foursome then joined by drummer John Densmore who Manzarek knew from meditation classes.

After Manzarek's brothers Rick and Jim made the incredibly poor career choice to leave the band guitarist Robby Krieger joined to complete the illustrious foursome.

Similar artists:

Jimi Hendrix
Janis Joplin
Jefferson Airplane
The Who

The band took their name from *The Doors of Perception* written by Aldous Huxley, which elaborated on his psychedelic experience while under the influence of the hallucinogenic and intoxicating drug mescaline.

Morrison's enigmatic nature and charisma became the heart of the band's distinctive sound, with a deep, haunting voice, poetic lyrics and uncompromising approach that set them apart from their contemporaries. His exploration of themes including love, spirituality and the human experience became the focal point of the Doors' music while his theatrical stage presence and unpredictable behaviour added a layer of mystique and danger to the group.

Fans and critics simply didn't know what to expect when they turned up to see a Doors show, which made for an exciting and captivating experience. On many occasions Morrison's evocative lyrics, erratic stage persona and confidence ensured the band remained synonymous with the counterculture of the time.

In 1967 the group were banned from *The Ed Sullivan Show* after Morrison ignored a request to change the lyrics from using the word 'higher' when performing "Light My Fire". In Morrison's defence, after already using liar, mire and pyre, the only real options were 'Girl we couldn't get much dire' or 'Girl we couldn't find a choir'. 'Girl we couldn't get more wired' would have had the same effect as the original line.

Singled out:

- "Break on Through" – Their debut single, with its dirty bassline and visceral vocals was not the breakthrough single the band hoped for as it peaked at a lowly Number 64 in the UK.

- "Light My Fire" – Ignited music lovers on both sides of the pond, written by Krieger with a sprinkling of lyrics by Morrison and Manzarek's catchy organ making it immediately recognisable.

- "LA Woman" – This is the sound you picture a stray dog has in its head as it merrily ambles along a pavement minding its own business.

Controversy didn't end there. In 1969 Morrison infamously instructed the twelve thousand-sellout crowd at a Miami concert to "get naked" while he was later arrested onstage performing at New Haven's imaginatively-named New Haven Arena in Connecticut. In subsequent years numerous states followed suit and banned the group from performing.

The notoriety of the band had little effect on the popularity of the Doors who built on the adage, or probably spawned it, that there is no such thing as bad publicity. In total the band released six studio albums over five years between 1967 and 1971, selling over one hundred million records worldwide before the death of Jim Morrison, after which the remaining members released three subsequent LPs.

Album of the week: *Morrison Hotel*

The Doors had been burned by a negative experience recording their previous album *The Soft Parade*, which took nine months to record at a cost of $86,000.

At the time of releasing *Morrison Hotel* the band was also still reeling from the consequences of Morrison's previous antics, which included performing intoxicated, indecent exposure and behaviour on a flight to see a Rolling Stones concert that saw a new law against skyjacking come into effect.

The Morrison Hotel featured on the cover was already in business in Downtown Los Angeles and despite not being permitted to take the photograph the band did so anyway when the receptionist was called away from their desk.

This, their fifth studio album, took only a couple of months to produce and saw them return to their bluesy origins with opener "Roadhouse Blues" becoming a favourite for cover bands ever since.

The only single released was "You Make Me Real", with the aforementioned "Roadhouse Blues" as the B-side. It failed to chart in the UK although the album did reach Number 12 and sold over two million records.

Jim Morrison passed away in 1971 at the tender age of twenty-seven from heart failure while in Paris. He was buried in the Poets' Corner of Pére Lachaise Cemetery.

Some would say Ray Manzarek and Robby Krieger sold the sanctity, if not the sanctuary of the Doors when they enrolled the services of Ian Astbury from the Cult to perform as the Doors of the 21st Century. The band performed from 2002 until Manzarek's death in 2013. Krieger was last seen uploading guitar tutorials for various Doors songs to the band's official YouTube channel during the Covid-19 pandemic. Meanwhile John Densmore is still alive and kicking, having married for the fourth time in 2020.

Your thoughts and reviews:

Billie Eilish

At just fourteen years old Billie Eilish was captivating audiences with her unique sound, candid lyrics and distinctive style. Her meteoric rise to fame is a testament to her talent and authenticity as well as her ability to embrace the changing landscape of the music industry. Her music blends the genres of pop, electropop and alternative music, characterised by eerie, minimalist production, thanks to her brother Finneas, while her distinctive, hushed vocals add a layer of intimacy and vulnerability to her sound.

Billie Eilish, whose full name is Billie Eilish Pirate Baird O'Connell, was born in Los Angeles in 2001. Along with her brother Finneas, who produces her music, the children were homeschooled by their parents in the hopes that they could pursue their own interests along with the normal curriculum.

Eilish first gained public attention with her second single "Ocean Eyes", taken from 2017's *Everything, Everything* soundtrack (a film so good they named it twice). The song was originally shared using SoundCloud purely for Eilish's teacher to download and choreograph a dance to but the internet did its thing and after several hundred thousand listens in two weeks it dawned on Eilish that a music career was possible. The single also featured on the debut EP *Don't Smile at Me*, with seven of the eight songs released to promote the record. Along with "Ocean Eyes", "Bellyache", "Idontwannabeyouanymore" and "Lovely" all charted in the UK with the latter reaching the Top 50. The EP peaked at Number 12.

Similar artists:

- Halsey
- Dua Lipa
- Lana Del Ray
- Olivia Rodrigo

Eilish released her first studio album *When We All Fall Asleep, Where Do We Go?* in 2019 at the age of seventeen. Subjects of the album included modern youth, drug addiction, heartbreak, suicide and mental health, which may appear to be strong for someone so young but unfortunately these are the themes that are at the forefront of Eilish's tender audience.

The singer continued with the tactic of mass releases, publishing nine of the fourteen songs from the album to a range of success. "Bury a Friend", "Wish You Were Gay" and "Bad Guy" all reached the Top 20 throughout the year while the album went to Number 1 across the globe.

Eilish followed up the success of *When We All Fall Asleep, Where Do We Go?* by becoming the youngest person ever, at the age of seventeen, to record a theme tune for the James Bond franchise. "No Time to Die" subsequently became her first Number 1 single while also making her the first artist born in the 21st Century to top the charts, in case you weren't feeling old enough already.

Two years after her debut album Eilish repeated the success with *Happier Than Ever*. Of the whopping sixteen tracks contained within, seven were released but with more success than the singles from her first album. Five of the seven, "My Future", "Therefore I Am", "Your Power", "Lost Cause" and "Happier Than Ever" all reached the Top 20 while the album, again, went to Number 1 around the world.

Singled out:

"Bad Guy" – If all the Looney Tunes baddies went on some ethereal car chase, pitting their wits to see who is the baddest baddy of them all, this would be the soundtrack.

"Your Power" – A track which showcases that, away from the heavily produced songs and with just her voice and a lonesome guitar, Billie Eilish owns an incredible talent.

"Everything I Wanted" – A song that makes you think of every wonderful thing that falls, like spring blossom, summer raindrops and popcorn bouncing in that traditional cinema machine.

In a short career Eilish has already received multiple accolades. These include seven Grammys, three MTV Video Music Awards, three Brit Awards, a Golden Globe and an Academy Award. In 2020 she also became the youngest artist in history to win all four general field categories at the Grammys in the same year.

Building on her astonishing success in music Eilish has used her platform on the world stage to shine a light on many political issues close to her heart. She has been praised for her authenticity and willingness to speak openly about her struggles with mental health while advocating for mental health awareness and encouraging her fans to seek help when needed.

Album of the week: *When We All Fall Asleep, Where Do We Go?*

Billie Eilish was only seventeen at the time her debut album was released, making her the youngest female solo act to chart at Number 1. The album went to top the charts across the globe, selling almost one and a half million copies, with half of the album's fourteen tracks released as singles.

"Bury a Friend" and "Bad Guy" reached the Top 10 while "Wish You Were Gay" just fell short at Number 13.

Eilish wrote the album largely with her brother Finneas O'Connell, who produced it at his small bedroom studio. It was not only the cheaper option but also had great acoustics, which suited the intimate record they were trying to produce.

Alongside the soothing vocals, the pair included sounds such as snipping scissors and dropping basslines guaranteed to elicit autonomous sensory meridian response, which is a pleasant form of paresthesia or tingling sensation.

The album's evocative and thought-provoking content based on Eilish's experiences of lucid dreaming, sleep paralysis and night terrors is enough to keep you awake at night.

Other issues raised include climate change and women's equality as well as subjects especially poignant to her audience. Her fashion is synonymous with oversized clothes, which she wears to prevent people from judging her body, while in 2021 she wore an Oscar de la Renta gown under the condition that the fashion house would permanently end its use of real fur.

In 2019 Eilish was named one of Time Magazine's 100 Most Influential People and was included as one of the BBC's 100 Women of 2022.

Your thoughts and reviews:

Elastica

Known for their infectious energy, catchy hooks and frontwoman Justine Frischmann's distinctive deadpan vocals, Elastica's minimalist approach to songwriting created tracks that were concise and to the point, rather like someone saying, "Well, if you don't know I'm not going to tell you". They left an indelible mark on the Britpop era, contributing to the vibrant musical landscape of the 1990s and paving the way for other female-fronted bands in a genre dominated by male contemporaries.

Elastica formed in London in 1992 at the height of the Britpop scene. Justine Frischmann and Justin Welch were both former members of Suede but left the band with a desire to make music that reflected the interests of people like them rather than things like dog man stars and love only coming in a Volvo.

The pair were joined in Autumn that year by Annie Holland and Donna Matthews to form a female-heavy quartet that stood refreshingly stark against the usual make-up of Britpop groups, which seemed to be made up entirely of lads lads lads.

Debut single "Stutter", released in 1993, didn't, and quickly saw the band rise to prominence especially when championed by Radio 1 DJ Steve Lamacq. Lamacq also happened to own the record label the group were signed to although BBC bosses were sufficiently hoodwinked by this abuse of power (as if the name Deceptive Records wasn't a big enough clue).

Similar artists:

- Catatonia
- Echobelly
- The Joy Formidable
- Sleeper

The band followed up "Stutter" in 1994 with "Line Up" and "Connection", both of which reached the Top 20. The latter brought them to the attention of the US market, featuring heavily on their mainstream rock radio stations and becoming a part of a further British invasion – a term which has been used sporadically anytime there is a glut of music from Britain invading the US Charts. Back in the UK however it was Frischmann's relationship with Blur's Damon Albarn that was making most of the headlines.

They released their self-titled album *Elastica* in 1995. Buoyed (or girled) by the inclusion of "Stutter", "Line Up" and "Connection", along with their biggest hit "Waking Up", released a month before the LP, *Elastica* entered the UK Chart at Number 1. With fifteen songs contained in just over thirty-eight minutes, its fast pace, high energy and witty lyrics captured the zeitgeist along with a loyal following.

Elastica's rise to fame was not without controversy. Accusations of plagiarism were rife but even in an industry that has now become infected with spurious comparisons of music, the similarities between the band's "Connection" and "Three Girl Rhumba" by Wire are undeniable. The same can be said about "Waking Up" and "No More Heroes" by the Stranglers. The disputes were settled out of court although members of the Stranglers actually spoke out in favour of Elastica, stating that similarities in music are inevitable while even thanking the group for reigniting interest in their band.

Singled out:

"Connection" – The subdued opening, which turns into a full-on aural assault, is like having someone throw a bag of fish and chips at you then scarpering.

"Waking Up" – No element to this song outshines the rest, creating a rolling three-minute road trip that implores you to make a cup of tea and put a record on.

"Line Up" – A crossbreed of Britpop and Grange Hill that just falls short of someone scratching their fingernails down a blackboard (three cultural references that may need explaining to the kids).

The band supported the release of *Elastica* with an extensive tour that lasted almost the entire year, taking slots at Glastonbury and the Lollapalooza tour along the way and visiting North America four times. The long schedule forced Alison Holland to quit the band, who was not replaced until Sheila Chipperfield joined the group in 1996, alongside David Bush who arrived after playing with the Fall (who hasn't?).

Working on their second album was no walk in the park, during which founder member Donna Matthews left the band, to be replaced by Paul Jones and Sharon Mew while Annie Holland returned to the fray. Appropriately titled *The Menace*, the 2000 release showcased a more experimental side of the group and although it peaked at Number 24 financial struggles forced Deceptive Records to close after which Atlantic Records, who Elastica had recently signed to, dropped them due to poor sales.

Album of the week: *Elastica*

Elastica's eponymous debut album crammed fifteen songs into less than forty minutes.

Singles "Line Up", "Connection" and "Waking Up" all reached the Top 20 while "2:1" made the soundtrack to 1996's lauded *Trainspotting* soundtrack, nestled nicely between Bedrock's "For What You Dream Of" and Leftfield's "A Final Hit".

The album was the fastest-selling debut since Oasis's *Definitely Maybe* and went on to sell more than a million copies worldwide.

While the likes of Oasis and Blur were fast becoming pastiches of the Beatles and the Kinks, Elastica's jagged guitars were more aligned to American new wave acts such as Blondie, so it was no surprise that half the sales of the album came in the US.

One can't help wondering whether, if only they had been more frugal with their songwriting rather than smashing everything out at once as if they feared the lifecycle of a mayfly, their career may have lasted longer.

Although Elastica's discography is relatively small their eponymous debut album remains a classic of the era. It stands as a testament to the band's talent, energy and ability to capture the spirit of their time. Elastica may have been short-lived but their contribution to the Britpop scene and aspiring female artists continues.

Your thoughts and reviews:

☆ ☆ ☆ ☆ ☆

The Fall

Associated with the late 1970s punk movement, in over forty years the Fall's music underwent a number of stylistic changes as over sixty band members came and went through a revolving door that could be used to power the National Grid. What has been consistent throughout is their abrasive, confrontational, repetitive guitar-driven sound and tense bass and caustic lyrics of the band's only ever-present and unapologetic founder Mark E. Smith.

The Fall formed in Prestwich, Greater Manchester, in 1976 after Smith, Martin Bramah, Una Baines and Tony Friel saw the Sex Pistols play at Manchester's Lesser Free Trade Hall. This was incidentally the same gig that inspired Bernard Sumner, Peter Hook and Terry Mason to form the band Warsaw, which was the precursor to Joy Division. Smith became the singer, Bramah the guitarist, Friel played the bass guitar and Baines, unable to buy a drum kit, bashed biscuit tins instead before switching to the keyboard.

Of the sixty-six musicians who came and went over the band's forty-year existence, largely on the whims of frontman and founder Smith, about one-third played in the band for less than a year. Reasons for members leaving range from the ridiculous to the understandable and include wanting to return to the cabaret circuit, disgust over the band's van driver wearing a Hawaiian shirt, needing to look after a dog and divorce from Mark E. Smith (in both a marital and musical sense).

Similar artists:

Gang of Four
Public Image Ltd.
Television
Wire

Smith had initially wanted to name the group the Outsiders but in a rare moment of ceding authority Tony Friel came up with the Fall after a 1956 Albert Camus novel. The story depicts a wealthy lawyer's fall from grace and while the band often teetered at the edge of such a demise it never came.

Throughout their career the band remained fiercely independent, releasing all but three of their albums on small independent labels. This gave the group complete artistic control and allowed them to pursue their vision without the constraints of the music industry.

The band recorded their first album *Live at the Witch Trials* in a single day, releasing it in 1979. From then until 2017 they released over thirty studio albums and numerous compilations, as well as live albums from locations that charted their sometimes stratospheric rise, as in *Live from the Vaults – Oldham 1978* to *Live from the Vaults – Los Angeles 1979*.

The period between 1983 and 1989 is widely regarded as the band's commercial zenith and coincided with Smith's girlfriend at the time, Brix Smith, being part of the Fall and bringing a more conventional sound and fashion to the traditionally unfashionable group. Covers of R. Dean Taylor's "There's a Ghost in My House" and the Kinks' "Victoria" reached Numbers 30 and 35 respectively while their own "Hey! Luciani" peaked at Number 59 and "Hit the North" hit Number 57. "Free Range" was the band's highest charting non-cover, reaching Number 40 in 1992.

Singled out:

"Lost in Music" – Up there with the best cover versions of all time, the Fall take the 1979 disco classic and turn it into an unstoppable juggernaut of house-driven indie sleaze.

"Free Range" – The infiltration of techno and dance influences into the band's sound is indicative of the way guitar music was waddling its way onto the nation's nightclubs at the time, baggy jeans and all.

"Theme from Sparta FC" – The soundtrack to a million grainy images of fighting on the football terraces from the late 1970s, this song is surprisingly melodic for something so shouty.

While never achieving high commercial success the Fall managed to create a huge following and influence on the post-punk and alternative music scenes of the 1980s, which I guess is the point. Meanwhile their influence can be heard in the work of countless alternative and experimental artists from Happy Mondays to LCD Soundsystem, all while joining the long list of groups cited as being "John Peel's favourite band".

In a tumultuous existence, the bedrock of the Fall was always to be found in founding member and frontman Mark E. Smith. Known for his confrontational and unpredictable behaviour on stage he would berate audience members and bandmates alike with nobody being above his vitriol. In 1998 he was given the NME's Godlike Genius award only to announce he thought the "achievement should go to the people who read the NME and can manage to read it from cover to cover".

Album of the week: *The Infotainment Scan* [E]

The Fall's only Top 10 album came at a time when the band were riding a perfect storm of high media interest while producing more accessible music.

The band aimed high, covering Sister Sledge's classic "Lost in Music" while aiming inextricably low by covering Steve Bent's "I'm Going to Spain", first performed on TV talent show *New Faces* and included on Kenny Everett's album *The World's Worst Record*.

Of the other eight songs on the original release, all were written or co-written by Mark E. Smith and contained the wit, both acerbic and subtle, that we'd come to expect, but that's what happens when you make a record in Rochdale.

While Smith denied that a reference to suede was not a criticism of the band but that of the material, there was little doubt where the lyrics of the ninth track "A Past Gone Mad" were aimed.

The album entered the charts at Number 9 while the single "Why Are People Grudgeful?", available only on certain re-releases, was also one of their biggest hits, peaking at Number 43.

On 24 January 2018, Smith passed away at his home in Prestwich after a long illness, during which time he'd continued to perform. After his death, surviving members formed new bands including Imperial Wax and House of All, which continue to release music and tour.

Your thoughts and reviews:

☆☆☆☆☆

Florence + the Machine

Fronted by the dynamic, enigmatic and ethereal Florence Welch, Florence + the Machine possesses an astounding ability to convey raw emotions through their music. Their sound harks back to bands from yesteryear while maintaining a contemporary feel that instils both nostalgia and exhilaration with each recording. Their songs have become a source of support and inspiration with many fans finding solace in the vulnerability and honesty of their lyrics, which encourage listeners to embrace their own imperfections and find strength in their struggles.

Florence + the Machine was formed in London in 2007 by teenage friends Florence Welch (Florence) and Isabella Summers ('the Machine'). The pair were joined by Robert Ackroyd, Dionne Douglas and Christopher Lloyd Hayden with many comings and goings along the way.

That their sound is so evocative of rock music of the past is paradoxically the thing that makes it sound so unique, sat among the heavily processed and soulless music that abounded when they first arrived onto the scene.

With early popularity bolstered after being noticed by the BBC's Introducing initiative, which looks to give unsigned bands a platform on which to air their music, initial support for the band was not misplaced. They soon built up a huge following, attracted to their poetic and evocative lyrics that delved into themes of love, loss and spirituality, all delivered via Welch's powerful vocals.

Similar artists:

- Arcade Fire
- HAIM
- Mumford and Sons
- Of Monsters and Men

The band's debut album *Lungs*, released in 2009, held the Number 2 position for its first five weeks in the UK and eventually hit Number 1 in early 2010 after being on the chart for twenty-eight consecutive weeks.

The album was preceded by debut single "Kiss with a Fist", which landed just outside the Top 50 while "Dog Days Are Over" peaked at Number 21 and "Rabbit Heart (Raise It Up)" went as high as Number 12. The album eventually sold more than three million copies worldwide.

While orientated towards indie rock the band soon proved they could branch out seamlessly into other genres. Single "You've Got the Love", a cover of the Source's 1986 dance classic "You Got the Love", reached Number 5 and at the following year's Brit Awards they performed with rapper Dizzee Rascal on "You Got the Dirtee Love", a mash-up of the same song along with Dizzee's "Dirtee Cash". The resulting single reached Number 2.

The group released its second album *Ceremonials* in 2011, which went straight into the charts at Number 1. The band again demonstrated the ability to cross over into the dance music genre by working with Calvin Harris on a remix of "Spectrum (Say My Name)", which became the band's first Number 1 single. That same year Welch also collaborated with Harris on "Sweet Nothing", which appeared on his album *18 Months*, joining artists including Kelis, Rihanna, Example, Nicky Romeo, Ellie Goulding, Tinie Tempah, Dillon Francis, Ne-To and Ayah Marar.

Singled out:

"You've Got the Love" – A track that regularly gets thrown into the Best cover version? conversation, it's only marred by the earworm of Louis Walsh regurgitating, "You really maydit yurrown".

"Ship to Wreck" – Built with flotsam and jetsam of the Cure, Fleetwood Mac and New Order this jaunty track has a sinister side if you delve too deep, like into the lyrics for example.

"Spectrum (Say My Name) (Calvin Harris remix)" – The obligatory mid-2010s collaboration with Calvin Harris demonstrating Welch's powerful vocals are a perfect foil for any genre of music.

In 2015 the band released their third studio album *How Big, How Blue, How Beautiful*, which this time peaked at Number 1 on both sides of the Atlantic. Singles "What Kind of Man" and "Ship to Wreck" were both Top 40 hits although two other singles released fell outside of the Top 100.

That same year they were thrust into the biggest of spotlights when the Foo Fighters had to cancel their headline slot at Glastonbury, leading the way for Florence + the Machine to take the stage and the plaudits while also making Welch the first British female headliner since Skin fronted Skunk Anansie back in 1999.

The band have since gone on to release a further two albums with only the fourth album *High as Hope* failing to reach Number 1. Their latest album *Dance Fever* saw them back at the top of the charts although this did not feature founding member and Machine, Summers.

Album of the week: *Lungs*

Florence + the Machine hit the ground running with their debut album. Buoyed by singles "Dog Days Are Over" and "Rabbit Heart (Raise It Up)", anticipation for an album was huge before its release in July 2009.

A cover of "You Got the Love" demonstrated the band's versatility, as did the White Stripesesque "Kiss with a Fist".

The album rides high on the incredible vocals of Florence Welch along with the writing, production and musicianship of Isabella Summers a.k.a. 'the Machine'. They were helped by production stalwarts James Ford, Paul Epworth and Stephen Mackey, who had experience working with Arctic Monkeys, Bloc Party and Pulp respectively.

The album has been reissued several times including an expanded version released one year after the original, a digital EP and a tenth anniversary edition.

Lungs peaked at Number 5 and has since sold over three million copies.

Florence + the Machine's success can be attributed to many things, from Summers' songwriting, Welch's vocals and the band's authenticity and willingness to push boundaries. Never content with adhering to a particular formula or conforming to industry standards they have fearlessly experimented with their sound, incorporating unconventional instruments and fully immersing themselves into a variety of genres to create a sound that is both endearing and enduring.

Your thoughts and reviews:

☆☆☆☆☆

Fugees

Whilst only enjoying a relatively short career Fugees are regarded as one of the most influential and significant groups of the 1990s. Their pioneering blend of reggae, R&B, funk and hip-hop created a new genre of alternative hip-hop, becoming the first act to break into the mainstream while being praised for incorporating live instruments rather than using samples. The group sold over twenty-two million records worldwide while group member Lauren Hill broke the barriers for female rappers to emerge from a traditionally male-heavy scene.

Fugees was formed in South Orange, New Jersey, in 1990 by Lauren Hill, Wyclef Jean and Pras Michael. Jean was born in Croix-des-Bouquets, Haiti while Michael is of Haitian-American descent. Their name was purposely used to take back ownership of the word often used derogatorily to refer to Haitian-Americans. The band also occasionally rapped in Haitian Creole.

What set Fugees apart from their contemporaries was their commitment to addressing social and political issues through their music. Their lyrics touched on topics such as poverty, inequality and racism, bringing awareness to these pressing concerns in a way that resonated with a wide audience.

They released their debut album *Blunted on Reality* in 1994, which fused elements of political hip-hop, jazz and neo-soul. It failed to trouble the charts though but it did feature the band's first Top 50 hit in the US.

Similar artists:

De La Soul
The Pharcyde
The Roots
A Tribe Called Quest

It was the band's second album *The Score*, released in 1996, that catapulted Fugees to the forefront of pop music. It peaked at Number 2, becoming one of the biggest hits of the year and eventually shipping over twenty-two million copies worldwide, making it one of the best-selling hip-hop albums of all time.

While the first single released from the album "Fu-Gee-La" just failed to reach the Top 20 the band went on to add their style and flair to covers or reworkings, all of which smashed into the charts. "Ready Or Not", originally by the Delfonics, reached Number 1, Bob Marley and the Wailers' "No Woman, No Cry" peaked at Number 2 while "Killing Me Softly", made famous by Roberta Flack in 1973, reached Number 1 in twenty countries.

The following year the band released the single "Rumble in the Jungle", which featured a whole host of heavy hitters including Busta Rhymes, A Tribe Called Quest and John Forté. The song peaked at Number 3 but later that year the group disbanded to work on solo projects.

Lauren Hill began writing and producing for a number of artists including Whitney Houston, Aretha Franklin and Mary J. Blige. In 1998 she also released the critically acclaimed *The Miseducation of Lauryn Hill*, which included two Top 5 singles "Doo Wop (That Thing)" and "Ex-Factor". The album saw a similar success to that which she'd achieved with Fugees, peaking at Number 2, with Eagle-Eye Cherry getting in the way of an elusive Number 1. Her album went on to sell over twenty million copies worldwide.

Singled out:

- "Killing Me Softly" – A song that inspired a hundred hip-hop artists into a musical career and a thousand drunken karaoke warblers onto the stage at pubs called the Dog and Duck.

- "Ready or Not" – Lauryn Hill's crisp vocal breaks into the haunting intro of Enya's "Boadicea" like an emerging swimmer, making for a chilling reinterpretation of the Delfonics 1968 classic.

- "Vocab" – With a bassline deeper than the Mariana Trench this is an onslaught of cool that takes the chilled-out approach of Fugees to a Spinal Tapesque scale of -11.

Wyclef Jean also began producing for a number of artists including Canibus, Destiny's Child and Carlos Santana. He has gone on to release nine studio albums with 2000's *The Ecleftic: 2 Sides II a Book* peaking at Number 5. He has also created the Yele Haiti Foundation charity in support of his native Haiti.

Pras Michael has also forged a successful solo career, releasing the album *Ghetto Supastar* in 1998. It peaked at Number 44 and spawned three Top 10 hits, "Ghetto Supastar (That Is What You Are)", "Blue Angels" and, along with Wyclef Jean, Queen and Free, reworked "Another One Bites the Dust".

Album of the week: *The Score* [E]

After their debut album *Blunted on Reality* stunted on release the band were given $135,000 and one last chance by their record label to deliver.

After buying recording equipment and setting up a studio at Wyclef Jean's uncle's house the result was a relaxed approach to recording that comes through in their steady rhythmic beats. Add to this the occasional outbursts in the background, not to mention the yodelling on the eleventh track "Cowboys" and the sound becomes beautifully spontaneous.

The album launched the alternative hip-hop style that came to prominence in the mid to late-1990s.

Of the four singles released only "Fu-Gee-La" failed to trouble the top of the charts, peaking at Number 21 when other singles "Killing Me Softly" and "Ready or Not" hit Number 1, while "No Woman, No Cry" just missed the top spot by one.

Although these hits were either covers or incorporated the heavy use of samples, Fugees added so much of their sound and swagger that they were doing much more than simply piggybacking on these hits.

The Score peaked at Number 2 in the UK, kept off the top by Alanis Morisette, but went on to sell over twenty-two million copies worldwide.

The band briefly reunited for a short-lived tour in 2006 during which time they wrote a track entitled "Lips Don't Lie". Disagreements within the band led to it being unreleased until Wyclef Jean changed the lyrics slightly to "Hips Don't Lie", took it to Columbian singer ShakiraShakira and scored a global hit.

Your thoughts and reviews:

☆☆☆☆☆

John Grant

John Grant is an enigmatic singer-songwriter who has captivated audiences with his unique blend of introspective lyrics, haunting melodies and deeply personal storytelling. This often relates to his sexuality, addictions and issues with mental health with a willingness to lay bare his emotions and vulnerabilities that creates a profound connection with his listeners who can relate to the universal themes he explores. Whether he is exploring his journey as a gay man, grappling with past traumas or examining the complexities of relationships, Grant's lyrics are filled with poignancy and empathy.

John Grant was born in Buchanan, Michigan, in 1968. The physical and emotional bullying he received in high school after the family moved to Colorado when he was twelve would later form the basis of his deadpan lyrics when singing about these experiences. Meanwhile his conservative Methodist upbringing was at odds with his sexuality and as a result he remained uncomfortable with this until well into his twenties.

In 1988 Grant moved to Germany to study languages and developed a taste for alternative bands. This would lead him in the direction of his music and upon his return to the US he co-founded the alternative rock group the Czars. Between 1994 and 2006 they released six studio albums after which the group disbanded and Grant spent four years working in New York as a Russian medical interpreter in a hospital and also as a waiter.

Similar artists:

Nick Cave and the Bad Seeds
The Czars
Richard Hawley
Steve Mason

Grant was persuaded out of his hiatus from the music industry by American folk-rock band Midlake and began collaborating with them on his debut solo album *Queen of Denmark*. Released in 2010 at the tender age of forty-one, this hugely personal album with tracks including "Where Dreams Go to Die" and "Jesus Hates Faggots" explores his struggles with alcohol and drug addiction as well as his struggle to reconcile his homosexuality. The album, which included Sinéad O'Connor as guest vocalist on three of the tracks, reached Number 59. O'Connor would later cover the title track "Queen of Denmark" on her 2012 album *How About I Be Me (And You Be You)*.

The singer followed up this album three years later with *Pale Green Ghosts*, which fared better than his previous offering and peaked at Number 16. Grant had since met Birgir Þórarinsson of electronic pop group GusGus who influenced the synthesised sound on *Pale Green Ghosts*.

Grant met Þórarinsson while on a visit to Iceland (the country, not the supermarket) and was so enamoured that he applied for citizenship. He would also go on to co-write the country's entry into the 2014 Eurovision Song Contest, scoring fifty-eight points and coming fifteenth.

He returned in 2015 with the Number 5 hit album *Grey Tickles, Black Pressure*. The album was his biggest success yet, peaking at Number 5 and continued to feature Grant using his songwriting talents as catharsis to all that he had witnessed throughout his troubled life.

Singled out:

"Down Here" – The uplifting strumming acoustic guitar lulls you into a false sense that Grant may break away from his usual melancholia, but thankfully the lyrics pull us back down.

"Global Warming" – A beautiful lament that has you Googling sassafras and Madeline Khan. Enlightened, your reward is a gorgeous rising organ sound a bit like Air at its most happy.

"Sigourney Weaver" – Here it is, saying what we've all been thinking all along about Sigourney Weaver as well as the casting in the 1992 version of *Dracula*.

Grant released his fourth studio album *Love Is Magic* in 2018. The record peaked at Number 17 and contained the same brutal honesty as before that jarred, in a good way, with an increasingly electronic sound. Meanwhile his latest album, 2021's *Boy from Michigan*, again saw him hit the Top 10 with an LP of introspective and autobiographical nature that the album title suggests.

Throughout his solo career Grant has enjoyed collaborations and friendships with an array of musical legends. These have included his aforementioned work with Sinéad O'Connor as well as live performances with Goldfrapp and the BBC Philharmonic Orchestra in 2014.

Album of the week: *Grey Tickles, Black Pressure*

Grey tickles is an Icelandic phrase for having a mid-life crisis while black pressure is the Turkish term for a nightmare, alluding to a more brooding approach to John Grant's music. And with this, his third album, the singer-songwriter yielded his highest chart position of Number 5 and his first Top 10 album.

The poignant, personal and caustic lyrics from the forty-seven-year-old bought an instant appeal to men who were in danger of cracking their necks while looking behind them at the prime of their lives.

The title track alone is among what must be, if you'll excuse the pun, a very small cluster of songs that talk about haemorrhoids. Meanwhile in the same song Grant references the gruesome scene in the early 1980s classic film *Scanners*, where Micheal Ironside's character causes a man's head to literally explode as his favourite, as if anyone had any other favourite scene in *Scanners*.

While there is a mischievous and subtle tone to the album, as if he's wondering if you're still listening, Grant also wasn't holding back and on promoting the album he appeared covered in blood and wielding a croquet mallet, describing this as how he'd like to react to people making derogatory remarks about his sexuality.

In addition to his years of success, John Grant's impact extends way beyond his music. His unapologetic embrace of his identity as a gay man and his advocacy for LGBTQ+ rights have made him a powerful figure within the community. Grant's openness about his experiences with addiction and mental health struggles has also inspired others to confront their own challenges and seek help.

Your thoughts and reviews:

Groove Armada

Groove Armada stand as a distinguished name in the realm of electronic music, celebrated for its innovative sounds, eclectic compositions and dynamic live performances. Comprised of the duo of Andy Cato and Tom Findlay the pair emerged in the mid-1990s to leave an indelible mark on the electronic music landscape. While epitomising the sound and spirit of chill-out their music went on to embrace a whole host of genres, blending elements of house, trip-hop, downtempo and dance music to craft a unique and versatile identity.

Groove Armada was brought to life in the mid-1990s after Andy Cato and Tom Findlay were introduced to each other by a mutual friend. Cato had previous experience in the music industry as a trombonist in the Grimethorpe Colliery Band while the pair bonded over a shared love of electronic dance music. After leaving university they started DJing at a London club called Captain Sensual at the Helm of the Groove Armada.

The dynamic duo decided their skills were attuned not just to playing the music of others but also to making it themselves and so packed a sampler and a keyboard and headed to a rented house in the Lake District town of Ambleside. It was here that Cato and Findlay picked up a compilation CD for 50p from a bargain bin in the local shop. The album contained Patti Page's 1957 single "Old Cape Cod", which references sand dunes and salty air and the rest is history.

Similar artists:

Basement Jaxx
Leftfield
Lemon Jelly
Moloko

"At the River" was to become Groove Armada's most notable recording although this was unable to help debut album *Northern Star*, which they released in 1998, climb any higher than Number 120.

The pair followed this up with album *Vertigo* in 1999. With this offering having a more mainstream and professional sound, probably due to not being made in a Lake District holiday home, it reached number 23 and was certified silver in the UK. As well as including "At the River", which peaked at Number 19 when reissued that year, the album also featured the singles "If Everybody Looked the Same", which reached Number 25, and the Top 20 hit "I See You Baby" featuring Gram'ma Funk.

Buoyed by the massive "Superstylin'", released in August 2001, the third album *Goodbye Country (Hello Nightclub)* reached Number 5 in the UK while bringing the band to the attention of the US Dance market. Single "My Friend" was also a Top 40 hit before further wanderings into a more eclectic feel took the form of 2002's *Lovebox*, which included a variety of genres including the jaunty reggae sound of the Top 50 hit "But I Feel Good".

Lovebox's high of Number 41 was disappointing but the pair returned five years later with *Soundboy Rock*, which peaked at Number 10. The album contained two Top 10 singles in "Get Down" and "Song 4 Mutya (Out of Control)", featuring Mutya Buena of Sugababes fame. The band released a further four albums of which 2010's *Black Light* peaked at Number 26.

Singled out:

"At the River" – Sand dunes are littered with coarse, spikey grass while salty air is, well, salty. Yet the dreamy refrain to this track that spawned a genre makes them both aspirational.

"Superstylin'" – Responsible for tidal waves of people hitting the dancefloor as soon as the intro kicks in, there is no prescribed way to dance to this.

"I See You Baby (Fatboy Slim remix)" – With lyrics referencing shaking asses this track was perfect for advertising the bulbous rear end of 2004's Renault Megane.

One of the things that sets Groove Armada apart from other electronic acts is its ability to create music that is both danceable and deeply emotional. In addition to their original productions, the pair have also become known for their remix work. They have collaborated with a diverse array of artists including Max Taylor, Neneh Cherry, Gram'ma Funk, Mutya Buena and Will Young. They are also renowned and a much sought-after pairing when it comes to remixing songs with a portfolio including artists such as Madonna, Massive Attack and Moby.

Album of the week: *Lovebox*

While not the greatest-selling Groove Armada album, *Lovebox* represents the pair's attempt to move away from the chill-out trap that they'd fallen into since "At the River" epitomised the genre and threatened to drag them beneath the surface with it.

The album peaked at Number 41, which was disappointing, nestled between the previous album, *Goodbye Country (Hello Nightclub)*, which reached Number 5 and the subsequent album *Soundboy Rock*, which reached Number 10. However, as an album in its entirety, it's an absorbing listen.

In a way the LP attempts to wrap up their previous work without the need for a greatest hits album (which they released two years later).

The sixth track "Final Shakedown" acts as "Superstylin 2.0" while the third track "Remember" rekindles the Balearic laid-back sound of "At the River" that oversaturation had left us far from fond of.

Instead of riding high on their previous successes a more upbeat approach resulted in a surefire way of getting headline slots at festivals, which worked at Glastonbury in 2002 as they played second fiddle only to Air on the Other Stage on Sunday night while Pink Floyd's Roger Waters and Rod Stewart were entertaining crowds on the Pyramid Stage.

The pair released their ninth studio album *Edge of the Horizon* in 2020, which featured vocal performances from Nick Littlemore, James Alexander Bright, Todd Edwards, She Keeps Bees, Roseau and Paris Brightledge. They toured for the final time throughout 2022.

Your thoughts and reviews:

☆ ☆ ☆ ☆ ☆

PJ Harvey

Not to be confused with chart sensations PJ and Duncan (the sensation being they actually made the charts) multi-talented Polly Jean Harvey can not only play a number of instruments, playing all but the drums on her sixth album *Uh Huh Her*, but is also a celebrated artist, actress, sculptor and poet. She has built a reputation for producing music that embraces female love and sexuality, setting new standards for women in rock while her 2016 album *The Hope Six Demolition Project* centred on injustices committed by the US for which she visited Kosovo, Afghanistan and Washington DC to conduct her research.

Born in the Autumn of 1969 PJ Harvey just missed out on the Summer of Love, although it probably didn't extend as far as Bridport in Dorset anyway. Her parents were avid music fans and introduced their daughter to the kind of artists and bands that would later shape her musical career.

Harvey joined Bristol-based Automatic Dlamini in 1988 where she met long-term collaborator and her musical soulmate John Parish. In 1991 she left the group along with Rob Ellis and Ian Oliver to form the eponymous (for her, anyway) three-piece band the PJ Harvey Trio. Oliver later returned to Automatic Dlamini with Steve Vaughan taking his place. After a disastrous debut concert at a skittle alley, the trio moved to London and things started to strike a little better.

Similar artists:

Bat for Lashes
The Breeders
Brooke Combe
Patti Smith

Debut single "Dress" failed to chart in 1991 but was still voted as Melody Maker's Single of the Week by John Peel. Album *Dry*, released in 1992, peaked at Number 11 and is said to be Kurt Cobain's sixteenth-favourite album ever while 1993's *Rid of Me* peaked at Number 3. The trio split later that year however, whereupon it would have been rather churlish of the other two musicians to lay claim to the band name. Touring with U2 on their global Zoo TV tour would be their final act together.

Harvey's first offering as a solo artist was 2015's million-selling *To Bring You My Love*. The album reached Number 12 and included three Top 40 singles, "Down by the Water", "C'mon Billy" and "Send His Love to Me".

The following year Harvey duetted with Nick Cave on the single "Henry Lee", the third track on the deliciously dark *Murder Ballads* album, which peaked at Number 36. In 1998 she featured on the track "Broken Homes", which appeared on Tricky's *Angels with Dirty Faces* album and reached Number 25.

That same year she released her own Top 20 album *Is This Desire?* followed in 2000 with another million-selling album *Stories from the City, Stories from the Sea* for which she became the first female solo artist to receive the Mercury Music Prize. 2004's *Uh Huh Her* peaked at Number 12 while 2007's *White Chalk* went one better. In 2011 she released her first Top 10 album since going solo, *Let England Shake*, for which she received her second Mercury Music Prize, becoming the first artist ever to do so.

Singled out:

"M-Bike" [E] – A funky insight into a three-way relationship between Harvey, her partner and his motorbike. The honesty in this track is both insightful and refreshing.

"Rid of Me" – Absolutely laid bare. A track that seems born from Harvey's desire to shout out her innermost feelings rather than the possibility of watching the royalties from a single roll in.

"Down by the Water" – Harvey's rasping voice competing with the dirty bassline creates a roving lament that trundles along like stream water over rocks and stones.

It would be five years before Harvey released another record, during which time she was recognised by the Queen and received an MBE for services to music. 2016's *The Hope Six Demolition Project* was PJ Harvey's first Number 1, which she followed up in 2023 with *I Inside the Old Year Dying*, which peaked at Number 5.

Not only has her music carved huge respect for her own recordings but PJ Harvey can also lay huge claim to the success of others. Record producer Steve Albini used his work on the album *Rid of Me* as his CV for getting the gig to produce Nirvana's third and final album *In Utero*. Meanwhile after her relationship with Nick Cave ended Harvey became the muse to much of the Australian's 1997 album *The Boatman's Call*. This included the beautifully lamenting "Into My Arms".

Album of the week: *Let England Shake*

Written over two and a half years then thrashed together in five weeks at a church in Dorset, forever a poet PJ Harvey penned the lyrics first and then added the music later.

The album initially entered the charts at Number 8 selling twice as many records as anticipated.

Following its win of the Mercury Music Prize in September it re-entered at Number 24 with sales increasing over one thousand percent.

Harvey was determined to create something different to her back catalogue to date while promotion of the record included an appearance on Andrew Marr's Sunday politics show. She appeared alongside the bewildered former Prime Minister Gordon Brown, which was unsurprising given the album's raison d'être was to force middle-England to take a long, hard look at itself.

More melodic and therefore accessible and almost cheery in places, to the general public (and watchers of Sunday morning politics shows) the album was lapped up both in middle England and across much of the rest of the world.

Over a career extending across thirty years PJ Harvey's enduring ability to embrace and learn new styles has led to a diverse range of music that has helped her express herself in numerous ways. Covering genres including alt-rock, art-rock, avant-rock, punk, blues, electronica, indie and folk it has been impossible to pin her music down and even harder to ignore.

Your thoughts and reviews:

☆☆☆☆☆

The Housemartins and the Beautiful South

The Housemartins and the Beautiful South both left an indelible mark on the British music scene. With their catchy melodies and insightful, humorous lyrics about normal people, they made a refreshing departure from the mainstream. Both bands demonstrated an exceptional ability to capture the essence of everyday life and human emotions that resonated with their audience on a personal level. Although they share a common thread through the involvement of lead singer Paul Heaton, each band had their own distinctive sound and style.

The Housemartins was formed in 1983 by neighbours Paul Heaton and Stan Cullimore (not to be mistaken for 1990s footballer, Stan Collymore). Various other members were to join and leave during the band's five-year tenure, most notably Norman Cook who later rebranded himself as Fatboy Slim.

With their close harmonies, infectious melodies and mix of political and social commentary the band broke through in 1986 when their third single "Happy Hour" reached Number 3. Taken from debut album *London 0 Hull 4* the album title was later adopted as a headline in the national media when Hull City's first eight matches in their inaugural Premier League season included victories against Fulham, Arsenal, Tottenham Hotspur and West Ham United.

Similar artists:

Deacon Blue
The Lightening Seeds
Kirsty MacColl
Texas

The band's only Number 1 came in the form of a cover version of Isley-Jasper-Isley's "Caravan of Love" released at the end of 1986. They followed this up in 1987 with the album *The People Who Grinned Themselves to Death*, which peaked at Number 9 and included three Top 20 singles.

The band split in 1988 with Heaton and Dave Hemingway, with a little help from their friends, going on to form the Beautiful South. Named sardonically after their northern roots the new band carried on the tradition of the Housemartins but with a more mature approach, often touching on the usual themes of love and relationships but including social issues such as nationalism, domestic violence and football hooliganism, all of which were conveyed through their clever and thought-provoking lyrics.

1989's *Welcome to the Beautiful South* peaked at Number 2 and produced two Top 10 hits in "Song for Whoever" and "You Keep It All In". Briana Corrigan, previously a backing vocalist on this, their debut album, then came off the subs bench (to keep the football analogy going) and grabbed the opportunity to join the band by the throat in time for their second album *Choke*.

Corrigan's voice helped create the band's kitchen sink dramas, which included their only Number 1 "A Little Time". It allowed songwriters Heaton and Dave Rotheray to feature female perspectives in their songwriting while the male/female vocal tit-for-tat added to the band's unique and charming sound.

Singled out:

"Happy Hour" – The title alone brings instant joy along with a masterpiece of fast-paced lyrics that will forever be attempted on disco dancefloors yet never quite achieved.

"I'll Sail This Ship Alone" – A defiant anthem for those on the wrong side of unrequited love and a definite accompaniment to gin and tears.

"A Little Time" – A story that is bundled and wrapped up in less than three minutes in the band's inimitable jaunty style, which more often than not hides a dark undercurrent.

Corrigan chose to leave the band in 1992 after album *0898 Beautiful South* had reached Number 4. This led the way for Jacqui Abbott to join in 1994 in time for the band's fourth Top 10 album, *Miaow*. At the time Abbott was working in a supermarket in St Helens, which would have been a perfect opening for a spoof of the Human League's "Don't You Want Me", but there you go.

The band released their first greatest hits compilation *Carry On Up the Charts* in November 1994, which was a huge success despite its reference to the dreadfully bawdy series of films that ran from 1958 to the late 1970s. The record hit the Number 1 slot and became the year's second highest-selling album behind Bon Jovi's own greatest hits collection *Cross Road*.

Riding high, the band's next two albums *Blue Is the Colour* and *Quench* both peaked at Number 1 with the former selling over a million copies. 2000's *Painting It Red* reached Number 2 although the band suffered difficulties in both promoting and touring the album, which included Abbott's departure, citing the pressures of touring and needing to look after her son who had just been diagnosed as autistic. She was replaced by Alison Wheeler who took on the female singer role in time for 2003's *Gaze*.

Album of the week: *Welcome to the Beautiful South*

The Beautiful South's debut album was an instant success, peaking at Number 2 and containing the singles "Song for Whoever" and "You Keep It All In", which both reached the Top 10.

"I'll Sail This Ship Alone" also reached the Top 40 while the album went on to sell over three hundred thousand copies.

The original cover showed the band's subversive side and included two photographs, one of a man smoking, with the other depicting a woman with a gun in her mouth. As a result, high street chain Woolworths refused to stock the album so an alternative cover was produced with a stuffed toy rabbit and teddy bear. The album is still available at all good record stores while Woolworths went bust in 2008.

In 2004 the band released their penultimate album *Golddiggas, Headnodders and Pholk Songs* with all but one of the tracks cover songs of other artists. These included songs as diverse as "You're the One That I Want", "Livin' Thing" and S Club 7's "Don't Stop Moving". The final album *Superbi* was released in 2006 and peaked at Number 6.

Paul Heaton left the Beautiful South in 2007 after which the band dissolved after almost twenty years, producing ten albums and selling over fifteen million records.

Your thoughts and reviews:

Hüsker Dü

Hüsker Dü was an influential punk rock band that emerged in the late 1970s, combining their initial heavy music with a more melodic, diverse sound of college rock to become the pioneers of alternative rock well into the following decade. They were one of the first bands from the American indie scene to sign to a major record label and establish college rock as commercially viable, paving the way for other bands such as Nirvana, Pixies and the Foo Fighters.

Formed in St Paul, Minneapolis, in 1979, Grant Hart, Bob Mould and Greg Norton first played together in a band called Buddy and the Returnables along with keyboardist Charlie Pine. However, aiming for a hardcore punk sound the trio felt that the keyboard sound didn't fit and so started practising without Pine before he was unceremoniously axed without so much as a "Timberrrrr!"

The band named themselves during a jamming session while trying desperately to remember the foreign line when rehearsing Talking Heads' Psycho Killer (Qu'est-ce que c'est). After bellowing out an abundance of three-syllable phrases they thought would work they finally came up with Hūsker Dū, to which they gratuitously added the heavy metal umlauts.

Originally the name of a Danish board game with the literal translation of 'do you remember?' Hüsker Dü could just as easily have been called Perudo or Rummikub.

Similar artists:

Minutemen
The Replacements
Sebadoh
Sugar

The band's fast-paced musical style pigeonholed them into the hardcore punk genre although this was not a route they were trying to pursue. The style actually came as a result of them wanting to play as many songs as they could in the short period of time given to them as an opening act.

Their more melodic take on the hardcore sound soon struck a chord with college students while lyrically the band delved into personal and introspective themes, which also resonated with a new audience of listeners. The growing support along with the contrast of sound made them perfect for college radio stations, which widened their appeal and created a perfect recipe for success.

In 1983 the band released their debut album *Everything Falls Apart* consisting of twelve songs that lasted less than twenty minutes. The third and fourth tracks "Punch Drunk" and "Bricklayer" barely scraped longer than thirty seconds.

The following year they released the double album *Zen Arcade*. Recorded in forty-five hours at a cost of just over $3,000 the record contained a more ambitious songwriting style with the final track "Reoccurring Dreams" lasting a full fourteen minutes, which is just five minutes and twenty-two seconds shorter than their entire debut album. Their record label lacked faith in the commerciality of the album however and pressed less than five thousand copies of the record. It subsequently sold out a few weeks into their promotional tour and remained out of stock for months afterwards.

Singled out:

"Eight Miles High" – A cover of the Byrds classic and a lot less mellow than the original with some screechy guitars, shouty voices and barely contained anger a sign of things to come.

"Don't Want to Know If You Are Lonely" – Their only single to grace the UK chart, it's fast and frenetic and worth listening to just for the insane pace of the drumming alone.

"Makes No Sense at All" – This is the kind of song you imagine is on repeat on the pub jukeboxes in the various paintings of dogs playing snooker.

The band started on the follow-up album *New Day Rising* just as *Zen Arcade* was released. It was subsequently issued in January 1985 just six months after that of *Zen Arcade* and with its slower pace and more melodic sound peaked at Number 10 in the UK Indie Chart.

New Day Rising may have seemed rushed, but it then only took a further eight months for the fourth album *Flip Your Wig* to come out. The band took to producing this themselves, and buoyed by the single "Makes No Sense at All" they were rewarded with the Number 1 slot on the UK Indie Chart.

In 1986 the band released their first album after signing to Warner Bros, *Candy Apple Grey*. Initially the band had been reluctant to sign to a major label although the negative experience they'd had with *Zen Arcade* forced them to rethink. The second track "Don't Want to Know If You Are Lonely" became the band's only hit in the UK while the album reached Number 140 in the US and a surprising high of Number 28 in New Zealand.

Album of the week: *Zen Arcade*

With twenty-three songs on their second album and the final one "Reoccurring Dreams" running to fourteen minutes, this double album peaked at Number 11 on the UK Indie Charts.

Singer and guitarist Bob Mould had lofty ambitions for the band, wanting to be bigger and better than anything previous or certainly something different, which the band achieved by standing at the forefront of the alternative rock scene.

The album was created in a whirlwind of activity, recorded in one forty-hour session with only two tracks needing to be re-recorded.

After another forty hours to edit, the album was ready at a cost of just $3,200.

As if this wasn't enough, as part of the session they warmed up with a cover of the Byrds "Eight Miles High", which the band released as a non-album track, whereas none of the singles on the album were issued.

The band released their final album *Warehouse: Songs and Stories* in 1987. It fared slightly better in their native US, reaching Number 117 while it became their only album to chart in the UK, peaking at Number 72.

New relationships, businesses and drug use put paid to the band during their last tour in 1987. Following the official break-up in 1988, Hart, Mould and Norton continued to make music as solo artists or in other groups.

Your thoughts and reviews:

The Jam

Iconic British band the Jam emerged in the late 1970s and left an indelible mark on the music scene with their energetic and socially conscious brand of punk and mod revival. The band's distinct sound and impassioned lyrics resonated with a generation of disillusioned youth making them one of the most influential bands of their time. Over just five years they released eighteen consecutive Top 40 singles, which included four Number 1 hits.

The Jam formed in 1972 at the Sheerwater Secondary School in Woking after founder and lead singer Paul Weller got a few mates together to create a band. It wouldn't be until 1977 that they released their first album by which time a number of members had come and gone. The final cut didn't include a young Gary Webb however, who auditioned without success but brushed himself down, changed his name to Gary Numan and had another crack in the business. The eventual trio of Weller along with drummer Rick Butler and bassist Bruce Foxton, who joined the band in 1974, went on to huge success.

The band's fast-tempo punk-rock sound was not uncommon at the time of the early- to mid-1970s. Rather than shun previous music like their contemporaries however, they embraced the soulful sounds of 1960s Motown along with that from bands like the Beatles, the Who and the Kinks to mould both their individual sound and look. Meanwhile Weller also took inspiration from literature going so far as featuring an extract from Shelley's 'The Mask of Anarchy' on the back cover of their 1980 album *Sound Affects*.

Similar artists:

- The Boomtown Rats
- Squeeze
- The Style Council
- The Undertones

The band released their debut single "In the City" in 1977. The record peaked at Number 40 and became the precursor to their debut album of the same name, which reached Number 20 on release in May. Their following three singles all had a global theme with "All Around the World", "The Modern World" and "News of the World" all Top 40 hits in their native Blighty. In a tactic that forced fans to buy their singles "The Modern World" was the only track of the three tagged to an album with the band continuing this method throughout their career with half of the eighteen singles never finding their way onto a studio album.

The success of *In the City* and their increasing following saw the band's record label clamour for more material so they took just six months to release their second album. *This Is the Modern World* was released in November 1977 and peaked at Number 22.

With Weller suffering a severe case of writers' block, or more likely burnout, the band's third offering originally contained songs written primarily by Foxton. Despite the bassist having penned and sung their second biggest hit to date, "News of the World", the record label rejected this in the hope that Weller would regain his inspiration. He did, writing all but one of the songs on the album and the band, along with their record label, saw *All Mod Cons* peak at Number 6 when finally released in November of 1978. The two singles "David Watts" / "'A' Bomb in Wardour Street" and "Down in the Tube Station at Midnight" reached Numbers 25 and 15 respectively.

Singled out:

"Town Called Malice" – Includes the Woking working class conundrum of having to choose between buying food or clothes for the kids. Forty years later people still face the same dilemma.

"Going Underground" – An anthem that could've been the theme tune to the Wombles complete with a key change that Boyzone would be proud of.

"The Eton Rifles" – The lyrics are delicious but present a bit of a *Blankety Blank* curveball where most people would opt for the more palatable Eton Mess.

Much like the Kinks in the previous decade the music of the Jam reflected the class divisions and struggles of working class Britain that the band had witnessed while out on tour. After *All Mod Cons* they released two non-album singles "Strange Town" and "When You're Young", which were both Top 20 hits. Their first Top 10 single "Eton Rifles" followed, from the album *Setting Sons*, which was a Number 4 hit in the UK while seeing their first success in the US.

Their first single of 1980 was due to be "Dreams of Children" although a labelling error made "Going Underground" the A-side, fortuitously giving the band their first Number 1 hit. Not wanting the gaff to define them the record was eventually credited as a double-A side.

To prove this was no fluke their follow-up single "Start!" also hit Number 1. Album *Sound Affects* followed featuring the chart-topper and also "That's Entertainment", which Weller apparently wrote in fifteen minutes after returning from the pub. This was not the cause of its relatively low position of Number 21 however as the record was only available on import.

Album of the week: *The Gift*

The sixth and final album by the Jam was also their only LP to hit Number 1.

Single "Town Called Malice" / "Precious" also peaked at Number 1 while "Just Who Is the 5 O'Clock Hero?", a track that lauds those ordinary people with nine-five jobs, reached Number 8 based on import sales alone.

The album demonstrated Paul Weller's desire to experiment with different styles of music, most notably his love of Northern Soul heard in the opening percussion and bassline of "Town Called Malice" and also using the chorus of the World Column's 1976 single "So Is the Sun" as the introduction to fifth track "Trans-Global Express".

This move away from their traditional rock / mod revival style caused tension within the group though and they disbanded nine months after the album's release.

The band's final studio album, 1982's *The Gift*, was their first and only album to reach Number 1 while spending sixteen weeks on the US Hot 100. It showed a band at the height of their game although unfortunately in October that year, Weller decided to disband the group.

While their career was relatively short-lived their impact on the music industry continues to reverberate and their distinctive blend of punk, mod and new wave influenced a generation of bands that followed.

Your thoughts and reviews:

☆☆☆☆☆

Joy Division

Despite their incredibly short career Joy Division exerted a massive influence and achieved widespread critical acclaim with bands including the Cure, Radiohead, U2 and Editors citing them as an inspiration. Their sound was unique with dark, brooding lyrics and a haunting atmosphere that set them apart from their contemporaries. Whereas the punk era was about anger and energy, Ian Curtis's lyrics dealt with themes of depression, isolation and alienation with his distinctive vocals adding to the band's gloomy sound that was synonymous with the post-punk era. Their iconic album covers and artwork also continue to be referenced and imitated today.

Joy Division was formed in Salford in 1976 when childhood friends Bernard Sumner and Peter Hook were inspired to create music after attending a Sex Pistols concert at Manchester's Lesser Free Trade Hall. It was the same gig that also inspired Mark E. Smith, Martin Bramah, Una Baines and Tony Friel to start the Fall.

The morning after the gig Hook borrowed £35 from his mum to buy a bass guitar and, along with Sumner and also Terry Mason who had also attended the show, the saplings of the group had formed. In search of a vocalist, the trio placed an advert in the local Virgin Records shop to which Ian Curtis replied and was hired without audition. The band's debut came in May 1977 under their original name Warsaw as a support for the Buzzcocks and John Cooper Clarke at Manchester's Electric Circus. Mason left shortly after.

Similar artists:

- Bauhaus
- Echo & the Bunnymen
- Editors
- The Jesus and Mary Chain

While the band found it easy to find lead vocalist Curtis, getting a permanent drummer proved less so. Tony Tabac had played the drums for that first gig after joining just two days prior but in June he was replaced by Steve Botherdale. His over-aggressive nature didn't appeal to the rest of the band though so they left him on the side of the road after asking him to check an imaginary flat tyre. After this, the group used the tried and tested method of recruitment by placing an ad in a music shop window. Stephen Morris was the only applicant.

They carried their initial moniker, named after the David Bowie single Warszawa, until early the following year whereupon they changed it so as not to be confused with the punk band Warsaw Pakt. Joy Division came from the name of a sexual slavery wing of a Nazi concentration camp mentioned in the 1955 novel *House of Dolls*.

Curtis was born in Stretford but grew up in Macclesfield and as a teenager visited the elderly as part of a school programme. Morris was born in Macclesfield and went to the same school as Curtis. He came armed with a machine-like drumming style that became a staple of the Joy Division sound. Hook was born Peter Woodhead in Broughton but spent part of his childhood in Jamaica before returning to Salford. Sumner, also born in Broughton, had previously worked for a Manchester-based animation studio under the name Bernard Dickin on the late 1970s cartoon *Jamie and the Magic Torch*.

Singled out:

"Transmission" – The vocals develop throughout the track hypnotically from initially stoic to emotive and deliver a crescendo so unexpected you emerge wondering where you've just been.

"Love Will Tear Us Apart" – A song that transcends any era and almost any genre that makes you think people will still be listening to this two hundred years from now.

"Atmosphere" – Never, ever, to be confused with Russ Abbot's 1984 hit of the same name, another hypnotic slow burner that's like ending up adrift on a li-lo out to sea.

Curtis remained the band's sole lyricist, writing the words independently of the music that was being created by Morris, Sumner and Hook. Their first recordings were heavily influenced by early punk and they soon developed a sparse sound that pioneered the post-punk movement and would later inspire the gothic-rock era of the early 1980s.

The band released their debut album *Unknown Pleasures* under Factory Records in June 1979. Initially they had signed with RCA but had dropped them after the label's insistence on using synthesisers. Without being preceded by any singles the album failed commercially upon initial release but eventually peaked at Number 5 when reissued forty years later.

In October 1979 the band released the debut single "Transmission". Originally recorded the previous year for the band's first album, which was aborted, it was re-recorded and claimed Number 4 on the UK Indie Chart while securing a Number 2 in New Zealand.

Album of the week: *Unknown Pleasures*

Tragically this was the only Joy Division album released during singer Ian Curtis's lifetime and therefore the only album we can say the band were happy with.

With no tracks released as singles, this was initially an introspective album and remained commercially unsuccessful, although the fortieth-anniversary reissue charted at Number 5.

The sound of the album was as much to do with producer Martin Hannett as it was to do with the band. Hannett wanted to create a different version of Joy Division's live shows and employed a number of innovative recording techniques on the record, which included smashing bottles, people eating crisps and flushing toilets, a bit like watching a film at Showcase cinemas.

The result created an album that leapt from post-punk music into the electronic sound of the early 1980s that many bands leapt upon to create their own sound.

The band were at the start of what could have been a glittering career, although the troubles faced by frontman Curtis overtook them. He struggled with many challenges including a failing marriage, depression and epilepsy. As the band's popularity grew and their touring schedule intensified his health made it increasingly difficult to perform and he began to experience seizures on stage. He died by suicide on the eve of what would have been the band's first North American tour in May 1980, aged twenty-three.

Subsequent releases included the band's second album *Closer*, released two months after Curtis's death and which peaked at Number 6. Compilation album *Still*, released in October 1981, reached Number 5 while *Substance*, released in 1988 peaked at Number 7, all lamenting what might have been.

Your thoughts and reviews:

☆☆☆☆☆

The Kinks

The Kinks burst onto the music scene with a blend of rock and roll and elements of British music hall with lyrics extolling life in Blighty, which set them apart from bands of a similar ilk who were taking the US by storm. Across a career lasting thirty-two years they sold over fifty million records and achieved nine Top 40 albums, five of which reached the Top 10 and saw seventeen singles hit the Top 20. Years after their formation their influence on Britpop bands in the 1990s is unmistakeable.

The Kinks formed in the North London suburbs in 1963 by brothers Ray and Dave Davies along with drummer Mick Avory and bassist Pete Quaife. An early string of lead vocalists included Rod Stewart while Avory had previously played one gig with an early version of the Rolling Stones. Former names included the Ray Davies Quartet and the Ravens but on looking for something a little more outrageous they opted for the Kinks.

Their early influences drew from American R&B and rock and roll but this soon changed after being refused entry to the US in 1965 and their subsequent inability to play in the country for four years. Ray Davies was therefore forced to look inwards and while their contemporaries were being influenced by worldly adventures encountered while they were able to tour the globe, Davies was creating a unique, humorous and much-loved lyrical style focussing on English culture and lifestyle that would give a more relatable feature to the band's music.

Similar artists:

The Animals
The Byrds
Small Faces
The Troggs

The band's first two singles "Long Tall Sally" and "You Still Want Me" failed to chart when released in 1964 resulting in their record label threatening to drop them if their follow-up single was a further disappointment. The band responded with "You Really Got Me", which reached Number 1 while their debut album simply entitled *Kinks* was also a success and peaked at Number 3 in the UK while reaching the Top 30 in the US.

The following year's tour was a disaster for the band. Not only had Dave Davies and Avory engaged in a fight onstage at their Cardiff concert, which rendered Davies unconscious, but similar bad behaviour in the US saw them banned from touring the country by the American Federation of Musicians. This effectively cut them off from the main market at the height of the first British Invasion – a term which has been used sporadically anytime there is a glut of music from Britain invading the US Charts.

The band's second album, 1965's *Kinda Kinks,* was completed and released within two weeks. It emulated their debut album, peaking at Number 3 in the UK while sales in the US naturally dipped. That same year they followed this up with the Top 10 album *The Kink Controversy* while in between the band released six non-album singles including their second Number 1 "Tired of Waiting for You" and the Top 10 hit "See My Friends". This track used a drone effect played on guitar reminiscent of the Indian tambura, which later inspired the Beatles' "Norwegian Wood".

Singled out:

"Lola" – One of those nutshell stories contained in a single with a chorus that's literally spelt out for you it's a surprise this hasn't yet made it to the football terrace lexicon at Bury, Hull or York.

"Waterloo Sunset" – A love song to London that meanders along like the river that runs through the city. It even manages to make the name Terry sound romantic.

"You Really Got Me" – Unapologetic. A song that builds and builds on the progressive "Oh yeahs!" that even the most reluctant karaoke star will be bellowing it out like Freddie by the end.

1965's "Till the End of the Day" began a run of seven Top 10 singles, six of which reached the Top 5 and by the time 1966 arrived their songs captured the very essence and commentary of pure Britishness. "Dedicated Follower of Fashion" peaked at Number 4, "Sunny Afternoon" and "Waterloo Sunset" came hot on its Cuban heels, England won the men's football World Cup and the whole world seemed bathed in the cross of Saint George.

The following year's single "Susannah's Still Alive" saw a turning point in the band's popularity with singles and albums failing to live up to previous sales. The band remained relevant though with the single "Lola", describing an encounter with a transexual, released in 1970. Despite a ban by the BBC put in place as the original version included a reference to Coca-Cola the song peaked at Number 2 once the lyrics were changed to cherry cola. "Apeman" then reached Number 5 but follow-up "Supersonic Rocket Ship" would be their last UK Top 20 hit for more than a decade as the band fell out of orbit.

Album of the week: *The Kinks Are the Village Green Preservation Society*

With no supporting singles released in the UK the sixth studio album from the Kinks and the last to feature the original lineup, struggled to make much of an impact when released. However, the album has since gone on to be critically acclaimed.

It is said to have influenced a number of American indie bands throughout the 1980s and 1990s as well as countless numbers of Britpop bands in their native Blighty and has since become their best-selling album.

The LP's concept, as the name suggests, is based around an English village green, focussing on the residents and, of course, a talking steam train. Meanwhile one of the record's themes is the concern of the influence the United States was having on English society. With the band still banned from touring North America at the time this may have been laced with a certain element of sour grapes.

During the mid-1970s the band experienced a fallow period in the UK although enjoyed fame in the US that had been denied them throughout the previous decade. Interest was reignited at home though when a number of bands including the Jam, the Pretenders and Van Halen started covering their songs.

During 1981 and 1982 the group embarked on a world tour which culminated with a performance at the US Festival in San Bernardino in front of over two hundred thousand people. The band's profile then saw another peak in the mid-1990s primarily as a result of many Britpop bands citing them as an influence, which can clearly be heard in the sound and lyrics of Blur while the Davies' sibling rivalry has more than been matched by the Gallagher brothers of Oasis. The group gave its last public performance in 1996 and disbanded in 1997.

Your thoughts and reviews:

Kraftwerk

Kraftwerk's pioneering use of synthesizers and electronic instrumentation throughout the 1970s laid the foundation for the development of genres including synth-pop and techno, making them one of the first successful acts to popularise the electronic music genre. They pushed the limits of music technology with innovations such as homemade instruments and custom-built devices. Their music continues to inspire and captivate audiences around the globe and their influence can still be heard in the work of countless contemporary artists.

Kraftwerk, translated from their native German as power station, was formed in Düsseldorf in 1970 after Ralf Hütter and Florian Schneider met as students during the late 1960s. Schneider developed a fascination with music technology and together the pair embraced electronic instruments including vocoders, which change the human voice into audio data that can then be manipulated, along with synthesizers and drum machines.

The line-up fluctuated like an amplitude modulation wave until Wolfgang Flür joined the band in 1974, originally from a band called the Beathovens (geddit). He was followed by Karl Bartos in 1975 to form the quartet most associated with the famous Kraftwerk appearance, that of four mannequins in the window of an avant-garde boutique or "Showroom Dummies", as was the title of the group's 1977 single.

Similar artists:

The Art of Noise
Brian Eno
NEU!
Gary Numan

The result was a robotic pop style that combined electronic music with pop melodies, repetitive rhythms and minimal lyrics. This sparse use of lyrics was also evident in the titles of their first two albums *Kraftwerk* and *Kraftwerk 2*. Released in 1970 and 1972 these were largely experimental albums but still managed to reach the Top 40 at home in Germany.

In 1973 Hütter and Schneider, still just a pair at this point, released their third album *Ralf und Florian*, which at the time could have easily come from the front window sticker of a Ford Capri. This time they failed to chart in Germany but did score an unlikely Number 160 in the US.

They released their fourth album *Autobahn* in 1974 at which point the band saw real commercial success. The album reached Number 4 in the UK and was also a Top 10 hit in Germany and the US with the single of the same name, reduced from its original twenty-two minutes to about three-and-a-half for radio consumption, peaking at Number 11. At the time this change in musical style combined with work on their visual image, whereupon they employed German painter, graphic artist and poet Emil Schult as a collaborator to design artwork and cowrite their lyrics.

The follow-up to *Autobahn*, 1975's *Radio-Activity*, was less successful but saw the band continue to move towards the electronic pop tunes for which they are best known. 1977's *Trans-Europe Express* reached the Top 50 with the aforementioned "Showroom Dummies" peaking at Number 25.

Singled out:

"Autobahn" – Meant to evoke the drive from Düsseldorf to Hamburg, even the twenty-two-minute version is ambitious given that Google Maps puts the journey at just under four hours.

"The Model" – If you asked AI to come up with a perfect pop song this would probably be the outcome with all the robotic, automatic and synthetic hallmarks that we came to expect from Kraftwerk.

"Tour de France" – Conjures up images of a dreamlike sequence of an alternate reality from the perspective of inside a zorbing ball overlooking bicycles, bubbles and boulangeries.

1978's Top 10 *The Man-Machine* saw the band repeating earlier success. The album featured the single "The Model" but while this failed to chart that year it would later appear in 1981 as the B-side to "Computer Love". Radio DJs preferred "The Model" so the single was repackaged and re-released as a double A-side and saw the band secure its first and only UK Number 1.

The album *Computer World*, released in 1981, peaked at Number 15 and was supported by an accompanying world tour. With band members rooted to their instruments, they made use of live visuals along with films synchronized with the music in a style that would pave the way for the massive stadium extravaganzas of today.

The band returned in 1986 with *Electric Café*, shortly after which Flür left the group. Meanwhile their last album, 2003's *Tour de France Soundtracks*, peaked at Number 21 and included two Top 40 hit singles "Tour de France 2003" and "Aerodynamik".

Album of the week: *Autobahn*

The addition of Klaus Röder and Wolfgang Flür to the duo of Florian Schneider and Ralf Hütter saw Kraftwerk's fourth studio album become the first to chart outside their native Germany, peaking at Number 4 in the UK in November 1974. It also saw their first single release, that of the same name, narrowly miss the Top 10 the following year.

The first side of the album is taken up entirely by the twenty-two-minute "Autobahn" although the UK single edit was a more palatable 3:06. Meanwhile only a small portion was played on American radio.

The album also saw a move away from their early experimental music, adding lyrics to produce a more pop-orientated sound. It continued to incorporate the early versions of industrial music though with the band still attempting to capture the factory sounds of the Ruhr valley and conveyor belts of the local mining towns.

Kraftwerk's influence on early electronic music is undeniable with musicians and groups including Gary Numan, Orchestral Manoeuvres in the Dark, Depeche Mode and Visage all citing their influence. They are also credited as being the architects of techno, attributed to the Belleville Three who fused their repetitive melodies with funk rhythms. "Trans-Europe Express" helped demonstrate to the emerging hip-hop scene the power of drum machines and synthesizers while Afrika Bambaataa sampled the track's melody on the pioneering hip-hop single "Planet Rock".

Your thoughts and reviews:

☆ ☆ ☆ ☆ ☆

Lady Gaga

Known for her distinctive voice, unconventional fashion choices and bold performances, Lady Gaga has become an icon and an inspiration to many. She has sold an estimated one hundred and seventy million records and is the only female artist to achieve four singles each selling at least ten million copies globally. She was also the first woman to win an Academy Award, BAFTA Award, Golden Globe Award and Grammy Award in one year. Meanwhile she is a champion for self-expression and inclusivity, using her platform to advocate for mental health issues and the rights of marginalized groups including the LGBTQ+ community. She has inspired countless individuals to embrace their uniqueness and to be unafraid of expressing themselves authentically.

Born Stefani Joanne Angelina Germanotta in Manhattan, New York, in 1986, Lady Gaga's interest in music began early after being encouraged by her mother to play the piano from the age of four. Gaga attended the Convent of the Sacred Heart Roman Catholic all-girls school in the city, where she was bullied by the other pupils for her provocative and eccentric behaviour.

An early record deal with Def Jam in 2006 lasted just three months before Gaga was dropped, after which she worked as a songwriter for Sony/ATV Music Publishing, writing songs for artists including Britney Spears, New Kids on the Block, the Pussycat Dolls and Fergie (the Black Eyed Peas one, not the ex-royal or former manager of Manchester United).

Similar artists:

- Kesha
- Demi Lovato
- Pink
- Sia

Gaga's breakthrough came in 2008 with her debut album *The Fame*, co-writing every track on the LP. Buoyed by Number 1 singles "Just Dance" and "Poker Face" along with the Top 5 hit "Paparazzi" the album hit Number 1 and sold over three million records in the UK alone. The album was later reissued as *The Fame Monster* in some regions with the addition of further Number 1s "Bad Romance" and "Telephone", which she recorded with Beyoncé, along with the Top 10 hit "Alejandro".

The follow-up album *Born This Way* was released in 2011 and was another Number 1 global success. It sold more than one million copies in its first week and went on to sell over six million copies worldwide. The album's title track, which peaked at Number 3, became a huge LGBTQ+ anthem while "Judas", "The Edge of Glory", "You and I" and "Marry the Night" all reached the Top 30 with the first two both landing in the Top 10.

Gaga's third studio album, 2013's *Artpop*, was another huge success, reaching Number 1 in the UK and selling over two and a half million records. Singles "Applause" and "Do What U Want" reached the Top 10 although the latter has since been removed from digital versions and future pressings of the album due to revelations made about R Kelly, who featured on the track.

A year later Gaga collaborated with legendary crooner Tony Bennett to release *Cheek to Cheek*, an album featuring songs by artists including Cole Porter and Irving Berlin, with the intention of bringing jazz to a younger generation.

Singled out:

"Poker Face" [E] – How do you make Lady Gaga cry? Poker face. Anyway, this song manages to throw quite a few music genres into a single track that shouldn't work but somehow does very well.

"Bad Romance" – A juggernaut of a song symbolic of Lady Gaga's approach to the music industry, which blazed into every radio station, shopping centre and coffee shop like a truck.

"Shallow" – Lady Gaga's passionate voice often gets lost in the pop bombast of other songs but alongside a simple guitar and Bradley Cooper's soft vocal it finally gets its stage.

Following 2016's album *Joanne*, which peaked at Number 3, Gaga worked on the soundtrack to the 2018 film *A Star Is Born* in which she also starred. Her acting was well received, the album peaked at Number 1 and Gaga added another six million records sold to her inventory.

2020's *Chromatica* was a return to traditional pop music and another Number 1 album. The single "Rain on Me", performed with Arianna Grande, also hit the top of the charts while the following year she once again duetted with Tony Bennet on the album *Love for Sale*, which peaked at Number 6.

As well as her huge influence on music Lady Gaga's impact has also been felt across the world of fashion. She is renowned for her bold and avant-garde style choices, often wearing elaborate and attention-grabbing outfits and consistently pushing the boundaries of what is acceptable or fashionable.

Album of the week: *The Fame* [E]

Lady Gaga's debut album was a global hit, topping the charts and selling over three million copies in the UK alone.

Of the four singles released only "LoveGame" failed to make the Top 5 with her first two single releases "Just Dance" and "Poker Face" hitting the Number 1 slot.

Fifteen months later she released an eight-track EP, *The Fame Monster*, which in some regions was added to the original album as part of a deluxe version. It yielded three Top 10 hits with another two Number 1s.

The two albums combined have sold over eighteen million copies worldwide.

The success was due in no small part to Lady Gaga's tireless promotion across the world's media, ranging from *The Tonight Show with Jay Leno* in the US to the fifty-seventh Miss Universe beauty pageant in Vietnam.

The record started a renaissance with electronic dance music and while at the time of release the title may have seemed a little precocious, a few years on it seems more like a premonition.

In addition to her careers in music, acting and fashion, Lady Gaga has been a great activist for LGBTQ+ rights and mental health awareness. Her non-profit Born This Way Foundation supports the health and wellbeing of young people while she is also an outspoken advocate for political causes, using her platform to speak out on issues including climate change, gun violence and women's rights.

Your thoughts and reviews:

☆ ☆ ☆ ☆ ☆

Little Richard

Little Richard is arguably the most influential artist in music history, if you're arguing with someone who knows nothing about music history. His career lasted over seven decades but it was his influence over artists, which range from John Lennon, Paul McCartney and Elton John to Jimi Hendrix, Deep Purple and AC/DC that led to his musical legacy that spanned a swathe of music genres not limited to just soul and funk. Meanwhile his flamboyant style and over-the-top personality helped to shape the image of rock and roll as the rebellious and anti-establishment genre we have come to love.

Little Richard was born Richard Wayne Penniman in Macon, Georgia, in December 1932. The third of twelve children he was nicknamed Lil' Richard by his family because of his small and skinny frame, and that his name was Richard.

Described as the Architect of Rock and Roll, his musical style was typified by frenetic piano and shouted lyrics. Meanwhile his onstage persona was outrageous, grabbing the crowd's attention with exuberant performances that took the charisma of the Pentecostal church and turned it up to eleven.

This overexuberance was far from welcome in his early years and saw him stopped from singing in church while his neighbours would often complain about the boy singing in the street using tin cans, pots and pans and even the steps of the house as percussion instruments.

Similar artists:

Chuck Berry
Fats Domino
Jerry Lee Lewis
Carl Perkins

Back in the mid-20th century Little Richard's high-pitched vocals and suggestive lyrics were seen as a threat to traditional values and many radio stations refused to play his music. Nevertheless he continued to push the boundaries of what was acceptable, paving the way for future rock and roll legends including Elvis Presley and Chuck Berry.

His career began at the age of fourteen when, working at the Macon City Auditorium in Georgia, Sister Rosetta Tharpe overheard him singing her songs before a performance. She invited him to open her show and the cash received for his performance made his eyes light up with dollar signs not dissimilar to Tom from the *Tom and Jerry* cartoons and a career was born.

While always prone to criticism Little Richard excused his outlandish dress sense as a way of ensuring that white people didn't feel he was interested in their women. His sexuality is however unclear as he fluctuated between embracing then denouncing homosexuality.

His music and performances appealed to all races and his concerts during the 1950s saw white and black American audiences become integrated at a time when segregation was still very much in practice. At this time white musicians were often employed by record companies to re-record music by black artists to sell (often in higher numbers) to a white audience. Richard would later receive a Rhapsody & Rhythm Award from the National Museum of African American Music for his role in bringing an end to this racial divide.

Singled out:

"Tutti Frutti" – After a few tweaks to the original risqué lyrics the simplicity of this debut was a surefire hit. For all the karaoke stars out there it's spelled A-wop-bop-a-loo-mop-a-lop-bam-boom!

"Long Tall Sally" – Conjures up every 1950s American cliché, from girls spinning around in floaty dresses to boys racing in those huge cars that Mr Miyagi gave Daniel LaRusso for painting the fence.

"Good Golly, Miss Molly" – Piano tuners would be queueing round the block to give the Old Joanna a good service after being bashed around playing this number.

Little Richard's popularity extended from the 1950s and into the early 1960s and included hit singles "He Got What He Wanted (But He Lost What He Had)", which reached Number 38 in 1962 and 1964's "Bama Lama Bama Loo", which peaked at Number 20.

Towards the end of the decade his career took a downturn though as he struggled with personal and professional issues. He turned to religion, from whence he came, and became a born-again Christian and on the back of this released several gospel albums throughout the 1970s.

He continued to perform irregularly but made a comeback in the 1980s, combining his rock star status with that as a minister, often officiating celebrity weddings including that of Bruce Willis and Demi Moore. Throughout this time his devotion to the church never waned, which came partly after seeing a bright red fireball following a performance in Sydney, Australia, in October 1957. He attributed this as a sign from God that he should repent from his wild lifestyle, although in effect it was the launching of Sputnik 1.

Album of the week: *Here's Little Richard*

Little Richard released a number of singles in the lead-up to 1957's *Here's Little Richard*, spreading them evenly throughout his debut album and also the record's follow-up *Little Richard*, by which time he presumed we knew he was here.

"Tutti Frutti", "Rip It Up", "She's Got It", "Jenny Jenny" and "Long Tall Sally" all reached the Top 40 with the latter being the pick of the bunch, peaking at Number 3, all this on what was one of the first rock and roll albums ever produced.

All singles on the album are limited to between two and three minutes long resulting in an album of twelve songs that lasts less than thirty minutes.

As with his other albums though *Here's Little Richard* failed to chart in the UK and was his only Top 20 album in his native US. Despite this it is still considered one of the most important albums, not only of its time, but of all time.

On May 9, 2020, after a two-month illness, Little Richard passed away at the age of eighty-seven at his home in Tullahoma, Tennessee. He received tributes from many popular musicians including Bob Dylan, Paul McCartney, Mick Jagger, Elton John and Lenny Kravitz, but it would be his influence upon the many musicians as great as these which would be his lasting legacy.

Your thoughts and reviews:

☆ ☆ ☆ ☆ ☆

Lizzo

Often it's not just the music that makes musicians an inspiration. American rapper, singer and actress Lizzo was born in Detroit in 1988 but moved to Houston with her family when she was ten. At twenty-one, after the death of her father, she lived out of her car in Minneapolis for a year while trying to break into the music industry and has since cited the musical culture of the city as helping her get a foothold in her career. Although an accomplished flautist Lizzo's music primarily incorporates hip-hop but is also infused with genres such as soul, R&B and funk-pop.

Lizzo was born Melissa Viviane Jefferson, acquiring the nickname Lizzo when she was fourteen after hearing the song "Izzo" by Jay-Z. She grew up playing the flute but while at Alief Elsik High School had also started to rap, having to choose between the two as people often find it almost impossible to do both at the same time. Having said that between 2009 and 2010 she performed lead vocals and flute in a group called Ellypseas.

In 2011 she dropped out of college and moved to Minneapolis whereupon she lived out of her car for the first year. During her initial time there she appeared in a number of bands while trying to launch a solo career. She released her debut solo album *Lizzobangers* in 2013 while still a part of the hip-hop group Grrrl Prty. The album, along with debut single "Batches and Cookies", which she recorded with former bandmate Sophia Eris, failed to chart, as did singles "Paris" and "Faded" released the following year.

Similar artists:

- Cardi B
- Doja Cat
- Megan Thee Stallion
- Missy Elliott

In 2014 Lizzo was named by Time magazine as one of fourteen musical artists to watch. *Lizzobangers* was re-released by Virgin Records during a year in which she also spent time working with Prince at his Paisley Park studio.

The second album *Big Grrrl Small World* was released in 2015 with Lizzo writing every one of the twelve songs herself. Again the album and singles all failed to chart and it wasn't until her third album *Cuz I Love You* was released in 2019 that she gained critical acclaim. This release was a Top 5 hit in the US, selling over one million records while reaching Number 30 in the UK.

This success saw a clamour from the public to catch up and previously uncharted singles were re-released. 2016's "Good as Hell" eventually reached Number 7 in 2019 while 2017's "Truth Hurts" peaked at Number 29. At this time Lizzo had also embarked on an acting career and five years after highlighting her as one to watch she was named Entertainer of the Year by Time magazine. The following year she received eight nominations at the Grammy Awards, eventually winning three in the process that included Best Urban Contemporary Album for *Cuz I Love You*.

Lizzo released her fourth album *Special* in the Summer of 2022 and saw it reach number 6. The album included the Top 20 single "2 Be Loved (Am I Ready)" while, eleven years after starting her career in music and with her tongue firmly implanted in her cheek, saw the single "About Damn Time" hit Number 3 in the UK and top the charts in her native US.

Singled out:

"About Damn Time" [E] – A song with all the ingredients for a funky soulful disco tune that should be as much a staple of any summer barbecue as burgers and beers.

"Good as Hell" [E] – An anthem of empowerment. You can picture a leading lady walking off into the distance at the end of a film leaving a fireball behind her.

"2 Be Loved (Am I Ready)" [E] – A song about self-love that would have you pulling the top down of your car even on rainy days, or ripping the roof off if you didn't have a convertible.

As well as forging a career in music and acting, Lizzo has become known for her body positivity activism. She often shares messages of self-love and body acceptance on her social media accounts and frequently performs in revealing outfits to challenge traditional beauty standards. That, and dressing up as a Hershey's chocolate bar at the 2020 BRIT awards.

Meanwhile she has also been vocal about her experiences with mental health, particularly her struggles with anxiety and depression. She has spoken about the importance of therapy and self-care while being a strong advocate and open about her use of meditation and journaling to manage her mental health. In doing so she has encouraged her legions of fans to seek help for their own issues and anxieties.

Album of the week: *Special* [E]

Buoyed by the Number 3 hit single "About Damn Time" released ahead of the album, Lizzo's fourth studio album and only her second to chart reached Number 6.

From an initial one hundred and seventy songs Lizzo somehow reduced these to the twelve songs on an album, which was the highest-selling LP by a female artist that year, until Beyoncé and Taylor Swift came along a bit later.

Intended to reach an older audience the album contains a mix of pop, funk, disco, hip-hop and R&B with Lizzo even collaborating with Coldplay's Chris Martin on the twelfth track, which is actually called "Coldplay".

All of this was attempted while trying to bring those fans who had come along for the ride since 2019's *Cuz I Love You* (which hopefully is an abbreviation of Because rather than Cousin).

The album continues to promote and celebrate those at the fringes of mainstream society although the singer did need to perform an about-turn after using an offensive term in the third track "Grrrls". After criticisms from disability groups, the lyrics were subsequently changed.

Lizzo has also raised the profile of the rights of the LGBTQ+, Trans and Black Lives Matter communities. Her music and activism have inspired countless fans to love themselves and embrace their own beauty while her performances have become a celebration of body positivity and self-love.

Your thoughts and reviews:

☆☆☆☆☆

Mazzy Star

Notable for their ghostly and ethereal sound, Mazzy Star captivated listeners with haunting melodies and introspective lyrics delivered through the enchanting vocals of lead singer Hope Sandoval and the wistful guitar of David Roback. Their music combined elements of indie, folk and psychedelia, creating unique and captivating songs of huge depth and emotional resonance, practically defining a genre of dreamy melancholy that went far beyond shoegaze and right down into the depths of the carpet.

Mazzy Star formed in Santa Monica, California, in 1988, from the ashes of David Roback's previous band Opal. Roback had already produced an album for Hope Sandoval's former group Going Home after being impressed by a demo tape given to him backstage after a concert. After a bandmate of Roback's walked out mid-show while supporting the Jesus & Mary Chain he barely hesitated in approaching Sandoval to fill the void.

Roback's original record deal meant he still had to supply a follow-up to Opal's debut album *Happy Nightmare Baby* so Roback and Sandoval toured under the name for two years, promoting what was to be their second album *Ghost Highway*. Sandoval was unimpressed with the songs, written mainly by Roback and former bandmate Kendra Smith and desired to start anew. The pair did so under the name of Mazzy Star, having been joined by Keith Mitchell, a percussionist for Opal who would play drums on all four of Mazzy Star's albums until his death in 2017.

Similar artists:

- Cocteau Twins
- Lanterns on the Lake
- Slowdive
- The Sundays

The band released their debut album *She Hangs Brightly* in 1990 and although it failed to chart it did feature heavily on American college radio and managed to sell over seventy thousand copies in the UK. While pleased with the new direction, the shadows of their past bands still clung to the album with the ninth track "Ghost Highway" harking back to the Opal days while the sixth track "Give You My Lovin'" was written by Sandoval's previous bandmate from her Going Home days, Sylvia Gomez.

The dark and introspective quality of the band's music combined effortlessly with their atmospheric soundscapes. The second album *So Tonight That I Might See* was released in 1993 and saw chart success in the UK, peaking at Number 68 while hitting the US Top 40. A year after its release the opening track "Fade into You" hit the charts at Number 48 and by 1995 the album had seen over one million records sold. Eighteen years after the album's release, the ninth track "Into Dust" spent four weeks in the chart, peaking at Number 47 after featuring on adverts for Virgin Media and the computer game *Gears of War 3*.

The band released its third album *Among My Swan* in 1996, which peaked at Number 57 and featured their only Top 40 single, "Flowers in December". The band then went seventeen years before releasing their final and most successful album *Seasons of Your Day* in 2013, which reached Number 24 and brought the band their first success across Europe.

Singled out:

"Fade into You" – The depth of this tune is akin to whale song with everything resonating like the ocean while Hope Sandoval's butterscotch voice rises like fireworks on a twilight horizon.

"Into Dust" – The kind of song that reduces everything else to a sideshow, becoming a soundtrack while you view the world carrying on without you.

"Halah" – Everything in this song aligns so perfectly, like Russian dolls, measuring cups that sit inside themselves, tessellated patterns or those pictures you used to draw using a spirograph.

The band's last output was the 2018 EP *Still*, which reached Number 27 in the UK Indie Chart while the pair promoted it with a three-night residency at the Sydney Opera House. David Roback passed away less than two years later from metastatic cancer.

The influence of Mazzy Star continues to be felt with numerous bands and artists citing them as an inspiration. They have left a lasting impact on the alternative rock and indie music scenes with artists including Lana Del Ray and Ariana Grande leaning heavily on their melancholic sound.

While as a band their output may have been sporadic the pair have collaborated with many musicians over time. Sandoval provided vocals for the Jesus & Mary Chain, the Chemical Brothers, Air, Death in Vegas and Massive Attack and in 2001 joined with Colm Ó Cíosóig to form Hope Sandoval & the Warm Inventions.

Album of the week: *So Tonight That I Might See*

After record label Rough Trade went bust following the band's debut album, *So Tonight That I Might See* might never have made it to light after all. Reading interviews you'd be forgiven for thinking this wouldn't have been unwelcome by the introverts who make up Mazzy Star.

The album contains ten tracks that are so deep they are positively subterranean and it was no surprise to hear "Into Dust" used in adverts and even less of a surprise that it took eighteen years to do so.

Elsewhere highlights include the beautifully lamenting "Fade into You", which featured in a number of TV programmes and films and was to be their only US hit, peaking at Number 44 while reaching Number 48 in the UK.

Never producing radio-friendly singles and with the band never really wanting to either this album acts as a gateway into the dreamy world of Mazzy Star. It sold over one million copies in the US alone and one hundred thousand in the UK.

Roback meanwhile would produce and record music with other artists including folk guitarist Bert Jansch and with Beth Orton on her 1999 album *Central Reservation*.

Mazzy Star's fragile soundscapes and ethereal vibes have made them a distinctive and influential presence in the world of alternative music. With their mesmerizing combination of haunting melodies, Hope Sandoval's evocative vocals and a dream pop aesthetic, Mazzy Star has created a sound that continues to captivate listeners and inspire new generations of musicians. Whether through the nostalgic pull of "Fade into You" or the atmospheric journey of their albums Mazzy Star has given an even further alternative to the genre of alternative rock.

Your thoughts and reviews:

Missy Elliott

When it comes to influential figures in the world of hip-hop few have left as indelible a mark as Missy Elliott. With her groundbreaking music, unique style and innovative approach to production she has consistently pushed the boundaries of the genre and in a fun, free way redefined what it means to be a female artist in the male-dominated music industry. Her themes, which include feminism, gender equality, body positivity and sex positivity have helped her sell over forty million records worldwide, becoming the first female rapper inducted into the Songwriters Hall of Fame and the first female hip-hop artist inducted into the Rock and Roll Hall of Fame.

Missy Elliott was born Melissa Arnette Elliott in Portsmouth, Virginia, in 1971. She had a troubled upbringing with her mother taking her away from her abusive father at the age of fourteen. The upheaval and move to self-reliance had a massive impact on Elliott, creating a strong, independent woman who was to later excel in a male-dominant industry that often objectifies and marginalises female artists.

Elliott's first forays into music came in the early 1990s when she formed an all-female R&B group Fayze. They recruited neighbourhood friend Timothy Mosley, more widely recognised under the moniker Timbaland, as the group's producer. It was the start of a partnership that would see Elliott and Timbaland go on to collaborate throughout her career while launching his collaborations with numerous artists in return.

Similar artists:

- Ashanti
- Eve
- Kelis
- Lil' Kim

The pair's innovative production style blended various genres including hip-hop, R&B, funk and electronic music, creating a unique sound. After Elliott's original group split, she and Timbaland worked together on music for other groups, most notably writing and producing nine tracks for Aaliyah's Top 40 album *One in a Million*. On the back of this success with Aaliyah, Elliott received calls from Whitney Houston, Mariah Carey and Janet Jackson within a single month.

This success opened the doors to Elliott receiving a number of offers of record contracts from a variety of labels but she remained reluctant to sign, having previously been rejected purely based on her figure. She held out and eventually signed with Elektra who offered Elliott her own label giving her complete creative control, not just over her music but also over her image as well as the opportunity to sign other artists.

Elliott launched her solo career in 1997 with her debut album *Supa Dupa Fly* recorded in just two weeks. It failed to trouble the UK Chart, peaking at Number 124 but did reach Number 3 in her native US while spawning four Top 40 hits including the Top 20 "Beep Me 911" and debut single "The Rain (Supa Dupa Fly)". The tracks were promoted with innovative music videos, in particular the latter track, which introduced themes never seen in traditional hip-hop videos at that time. The LP eventually sold over two and a half million records worldwide.

Singled out:

"Work It" – Missy Elliot flips the usual misogyny associated with rap music on its head in a track packed full of delightful euphemisms and elephant trumpets.

"4 My People" [E] – The traditional 'This is for my mother' opener is a little bit of misdirection when given the time to finish the full sentence (not that you'd play this track to your mum).

"Get Ur Freak On" [E] – A track that leans heavily on a bhangra sound reminiscent of Knight Rider, spanning musical genres and becoming a nightclub staple ever since.

Elliott's second album *Da Real World*, released in 1999, peaked at Number 42 with singles "All n My Grill" and "Hot Boyz" both reaching the Top 20. The album eventually sold over six million copies globally. Her next release, 2001's *Miss E... So Addictive* sold over five million copies, reaching Number 10 in the process while the single "Get Ur Freak On", released ahead of the album, leaned heavily on a bhangra sound that spanned not just musical genres but cultures and became a global hit.

2002's *Under Construction* took on more of an old-school sound while also taking a bit of a downturn, peaking at Number 23. It did feature Top 10 singles "Work It" and "Gossip Folks" though. The following year *This Is Not a Test!* was less successful, peaking at Number 47. Elliott continued to find success writing and producing for a huge number of artists across a multitude of genres including Ariana Grande, Janet Jackson and Lizzo. Her final studio album *The Cookbook* did fare better, reaching the Top 40 and spawning the Top 10 single "Lose Control".

Album of the week: *Miss E...So Addictive* [E]

Missy Elliott's third studio album reached the Top 10 in the UK, containing two Top 5 singles "Get Ur Freak On" and "4 My People", along with Top 10 hit "One Minute Man", the latter of which was a prime example of Elliott turning the male-dominated and highly misogynistic culture of hip-hop on its head.

The album walked a tightrope over hip-hop and club sounds, taking influences from older and non-Western music and featuring an array of guest artists.

Elliott co-wrote all but one of the eighteen tracks on the album while also co-producing them all, along with long-time collaborator Timbaland who, at the time, was solidifying his reputation as one of the best and most sought-after producers around.

The album was an instant hit selling over two hundred and fifty thousand records in the US in its first week alone and eventually selling over three hundred thousand in the UK and over five million worldwide.

Missy Elliott has not only enjoyed a glittering solo career but has written and produced some of the greatest hits over the last thirty years. Meanwhile her influence on future generations of artists cannot be overstated. Her pioneering spirit has inspired countless musicians and performers to push their own boundaries and explore new creative territories. Artists like Beyoncé, Rihanna and Cardi B have all cited Missy Elliott as being a major influence on their careers while her ability to blend musical genres and defy expectations has paved the way for a more inclusive and diverse landscape across the music industry.

Your thoughts and reviews:

☆☆☆☆☆

Nirvana

Led by their enigmatic frontman Kurt Cobain, Nirvana burst onto the music scene with a raw and energetic sound, catalysing the grunge movement and bringing alternative rock to the mainstream. Their explosive performances and thought-provoking lyrics with themes of abjection and alienation brought them global popularity, which although only releasing three albums, helped them to sell over seventy-five million records worldwide.

The seeds of Nirvana were formed in 1987 when lead singer and guitarist Kurt Cobain met bassist Krist Novoselic while at school in Aberdeen, Washington. Such is their global appeal the town's welcoming sign now reads Welcome to Aberdeen. Come as you are.

Cobain initially approached Novoselic with a demo entitled *Fecal Matter*, which his potential bandmate understandably took a while to listen to, but once he did he was sold with the pair starting as a Creedence Clearwater Revival tribute band. The band played under the name Nirvana for the first time in March 1988 whereupon they went through a succession of drummers before recruiting Dave Grohl in 1990.

Cobain's introspective and often dark lyrics explored themes of alienation, depression and societal disillusionment, which combined with his distinctive voice and impassioned delivery gave the band a unique and captivating sound that struck a chord with disenchanted youth.

Similar artists:

Hüsker Dü
Pixies
Smashing Pumpkins
Soundgarden

Nirvana released their debut album *Bleach* in 1989, featuring drummer Chad Channing. The record soon became a favourite of college radio stations and so Cobain was understandably angered by their record label's inability to promote and distribute the album. Initially *Bleach* sold forty thousand copies in the US, which shot up to almost two million after they released *Nevermind*.

While Cobain's songwriting played a pivotal role it was the chemistry and musicianship of the entire band that were instrumental to Nirvana's success. Krist Novoselic's melodic basslines were key and when drummer Dave Grohl joined his input provided a solid foundation for Cobain's song structures and allowed the music to shine.

Still smarting from their experience with the distribution of *Bleach* the band signed with DGC Records in advance of their second album *Nevermind*, released in 1991. The label's initial ambitions were to sell two hundred and fifty thousand copies but on the back of singles "Smells Like Teen Spirit", "Come as You Are", "Lithium" and "In Bloom" eventually sales topped over thirty million.

The label was keen to follow up on this incredible success and so released a compilation album *Incesticide* in 1992, which contained a collection of various rare Nirvana recordings and peaked at Number 14. Their highly-anticipated third studio album *In Utero* was released in 1993 and topped both the US and UK Charts selling over fifteen million records.

Singled out:

- "Smells Like Teen Spirit" – One of the most recognisable songs ever recorded with a myriad of misheard lyrics shouted into in the sweaty nightclub brawls whenever it was played.

- "Heart-Shaped Box" – A broody, contemplative offering more attuned to Kurt Cobain's introspective nature than the more shouty tracks that the band produced.

- "Lithium" – Begins with a jaunty stroll akin to someone walking along the beachfront with a big fat smile before an itinerant seagull flies down and grabs your chips.

At the time the band were not only one of the biggest names in the industry but one of the most popular that had been around for an age. Pictures of the band, in particular that of Cobain and his tortured soul look, were becoming iconic. In 1994 however, he took his own life at the age of twenty-seven.

Following his death and the band's dissolution DGC Records released a recording of the group's *MTV Unplugged* show that the band had performed in 1993. Despite featuring a number of cover versions and being light on many of the band's greatest hits including "Smells Like Teen Spirit", "Lithium" and "Heart-Shaped Box" it peaked at Number 1 in many countries including the UK. Further releases have been overseen by the surviving members of Nirvana, along with Cobain's widow Courtney Love.

Album of the week: *Nevermind* [E]

Nirvana's second studio album fared less well in the UK than elsewhere around the world, reversing the relative success of its debut album *Bleach* in this country.

Nevermind peaked at Number 5 while singles "Smells Like Teen Spirit" and "Come as You Are" reached the Top 10. "Lithium" hit Number 11 while "In Bloom" stuttered to Number 28.

The global appeal was much bigger and the band excelled their record label's initial hope of selling two hundred and fifty thousand copies of the album by eventually selling over thirty million records worldwide.

The move to a mainstream label resulted in an album that was more melodic than their previous offering while also being influenced by the bands that Kurt Cobain was listening to at the time, which included REM and Pixies. The album also contains acoustic ballads while eclecticism was completed with punk-inspired hard rock. Meanwhile the front cover, one of the most famous record sleeves ever produced, was not without controversy and saw the naked baby pictured later file a lawsuit against the band, which was eventually ruled against.

Nirvana's impact across the globe reached far beyond their music. They symbolized a cultural shift and gave a voice to a generation, especially in their native US, that felt marginalised and misunderstood. They became the face of the grunge movement and saw the subgenre of rock, characterised by its distorted guitars, anguished lyrics and anti-establishment attitude, leap out from neighbouring Seattle and encompass the world.

Your thoughts and reviews:

Sinéad O'Connor

Sinéad O'Connor is one of the most recognisable and outspoken female artists to have emerged in music. She is known for her powerful voice, emotional lyrics and unique distinctive sound, creating a discography of the most evocative records in a career spanning over thirty-five years. She has used her music not just to entertain but also to address issues such as domestic violence, child abuse, human rights and organised religion while admirably bringing her battles with mental health into the public discourse.

Sinéad O'Connor was born in Dublin in 1966 and named after the Irish children's author Sinéad de Valera. In 2017 however, she changed her legal name to Magda Davitt to distance herself from her parents. A year later she converted to Islam and changed her name again, this time to Shuhada Sadaqat although continued to record and perform under her birth name.

Her early life was one filled with trauma. At the age of fifteen, she was placed in one of Ireland's now-infamous Magdalene asylums for eighteen months after a spate of shoplifting and truancy. When she was eighteen her mother was killed in a car accident.

O'Connor's music career began with a stint in the band Ton Ton Macoute, formed in 1984. While unsuccessful this did bring her to the attention of Fachtna O'Ceallaigh, the former head of U2's Mother Records, through which she co-wrote and sang with the Edge on the 1986 single "Heroine".

Similar artists:

10,000 Maniacs
Annie Lennox
Tanita Tikaram
Suzanne Vega

O'Connor released her debut album *The Lion and the Cobra* in 1987 and hit the charts across the world, eventually selling over two and a half million records. It peaked at Number 27 in the UK, reaching as high as Number 3 in her native Ireland, while her single "Mandinka" brought her to the attention of American audiences ensuring a Top 40 album across the pond as well.

The LP was followed in 1990 with the album *I Do Not Want What I Haven't Got*. In the lead-up to its April release, O'Connor scored a massive global Number 1 with a cover of Prince's "Nothing Compares 2 U". The album did likewise and sold over seven million copies while earning her a nomination for Best Female Rock Vocal Performance at the Grammys.

O'Connor's next album, 1992's *Am I Not Your Girl?* was a collection of jazz covers harking back to the music that she listened to while growing up. The release hit controversy however with O'Connor using her platform to highlight issues such as addiction and sexual and emotional abuse, therefore losing some of her global momentum. The album did however reach Number 6.

The following three albums saw a continuation of this decline and while *Universal Mother* entered the Top 20, neither 2000's *Faith and Courage* nor 2002's *Sean-Nós Nua* reached the Top 40. O'Connor did see a resurgence in popularity in 2012 with the release of *How About I Be Me (and You Be You)?* which peaked at Number 33 while her final album, 2014's *I'm Not Bossy, I'm the Boss* reached Number 22 and topped the charts back at her home.

Singled out:

- "Nothing Compares 2 U" – A heartbreakingly stunning reinterpretation of the original song written by Prince that's probably the greatest cover song ever.

- "Mandinka" – A big college radio hit in the US, unsurprising as it comes complete with one of those choruses you can sing along to with words you've made up yourself.

- "Success Has Made a Failure of Our Home" – Beginning on a wave of orchestral rises before giving way to a powerful jazz crescendo this could easily be a James Bond theme.

Throughout her career Sinéad O'Connor has never been afraid to speak openly about her spirituality as well as air her social and political views. She has also been candid about her personal struggles with depression and mental health and in 2017 appeared on American TV in order to destigmatise mental illness.

She continued to raise issues using actions as well as the words of her music to raise their profile and ensure people were made aware of these rather than remain silent. Her early shaven-headed appearance was based on her assertion against traditional views of women and in particular the image her record label wanted to portray while she refused to perform in venues where the country's national anthem was played prior to concerts.

Album of the week: *I Do Not Want What I Haven't Got*

Sinéad O'Connor's second studio album, featuring the iconic cover of Prince's "Nothing Compares 2 U", peaked at Number 1 around the world. Originally written as an ode to unrequited love, O'Connor sang the song in relation to the complicated relationship with her mother who had passed away five years earlier.

The artist was in high demand but instead of using the opportunity offered by media interviews to promote the album, she instead used her newfound fame and celebrity to speak out against a range of social injustices. Despite this, or because of it, the album sold over seven million copies worldwide.

The album opens with the "Serenity Prayer", which asks for "the serenity to accept the things I cannot change, the courage to change the things I can, and the wisdom to know the difference". It was an insight into a troubled mindset that would continue to be a dominating factor throughout her career. Elsewhere on the album, eclecticism was complete when O'Connor added a sample of James Brown's "Funky Drummer" onto her rendition of the 17th century Irish poem "I Am Stretched on Your Grave".

O'Connor's most infamous act came in 1992 when she tore a picture of Pope John Paul II live on American TV despite knowing that this would damage her career. The act was misinterpreted as an attack against the church while in effect it was her way of protesting about sexual abuse within and the coverups that were being put in place. It wasn't until eighteen years later that Pope Benedict XVI issued an apology to the victims of decades of sexual abuse by Catholic priests in Ireland.

In July 2023 Sinéad O'Connor was found unresponsive at her flat in South London and had passed away from natural causes. She was fifty-six years old.

Your thoughts and reviews:

☆☆☆☆☆

Dolly Parton

Beginning in the mid-1960s Dolly Parton's career has spanned almost sixty years and resulted in sixty-six albums and over three thousand songs. She has sold more than one hundred million records worldwide, making her one of the best-selling female artists of all time. While mostly associated with country music Dolly Parton has also released a number of crossover hits that made the mainstream. In addition she has become an accomplished actor while her acts of philanthropy have helped countless people in her native US.

Dolly Parton was born in 1946 in a one-room cabin on the banks of the Little Pigeon River in Pittman Center, Tennessee. She had eleven siblings, with her mother pushing out children with as much gusto as Dolly would later release albums. By the age of seven, she had started playing a homemade guitar and would later be gifted one by her uncle while as a child she also made appearances on local radio and TV programmes.

Dolly signed with Monument Records in 1965 but while her heart was in making country music the label disagreed and believed her unique soprano voice was more suited to pop. The following year however she co-wrote the song "Put It Off Until Tomorrow" with her uncle Bill Owens, upon which she sang the harmony on the demo. When this was offered to Bill Phillips to record he was adamant that he wanted whoever sang those harmonies to appear on the record, which Parton subsequently did, generating widespread interest among country radio listeners and therefore the label relented.

Similar artists:

Emmylou Harris
Loretta Lynn
Crystal Gayle
Tammy Wynette

Parton released her debut album, *Hello, I'm Dolly* in 1967 but saw her first six albums confined to the US Country Charts. Monument Records were still calling the shots and insisted her records were duets performed with Porter Wagoner and in June 1970 he persuaded her to record "Mule Skinner Blues", which reached Number 3 in the US Country Chart. She followed this with her first Country Number 1 "Joshua" in November, with the album of the same name just climbing into the US Charts the following year.

1973 saw "Jolene" become Parton's first record to break into the US Singles Chart while eventually peaking at Number 7 in the UK in 1976. The follow-up single "I Will Always Love You" failed to reach either pop chart, although when Whitney Houston covered the song in 1992 for *the Bodyguard* soundtrack it went to Number 1 around the world and sold twenty million copies. Meanwhile Elvis Presley had indicated a previous desire to record the song although when told that he would receive half the publishing rights Parton rightly refused.

Parton's albums continued to chart highly in the Country Chart without much mainstream impact. That was until 1977's *New Harvest...First Gathering* reached Number 71 in the US and following this, she began releasing music that appealed to listeners of both country and pop. 1977's "Here You Come Again" reached Number 3 in the US and Number 75 in the UK while the album of the same name became her first million-seller.

Singled out:

- "I Will Always Love You" – Whitney Houston's lungs and vocal chords brought this song to international prominence but the charm and elegance of the original deserves its own standing.

- "Jolene" – A song that utilises Dolly Parton's accent to best effect when rhyming men and again, spawning one of the world's most famous names (although I've never met a woman called Jolene).

- "9 to 5" – One of those tracks that third-rate wedding DJs keep on hand for when the dancefloor gets particularly sparse. 2 Many DJs' mash-up of this with Röyksopp's "Eple" is worth a listen.

Parton's commercial success grew in 1980 with three consecutive Country Chart Number 1 hits culminating in "9 to 5" reaching Number 1 in the US and the Top 50 in the UK. 1983's "Islands in The Stream", written by the Bee Gees and recorded with Kenny Rogers, reached Number 7 in the UK while in 1987 she teamed up with Emmylou Harris and Linda Ronstadt to record the album *Trio*, which sold over one million copies and catapulted her back into the public's consciousness.

It wasn't until the mid-1990s that Dolly Parton started to see continued success in the UK however. Album *Treasures*, released in 1996, was the first to chart in the UK with follow-up *Hungry Again* peaking at Number 41. The following decade five of her six albums reached the Top 40.

The 2010s arrived but rather than take her foot off the gas Parton's appeal only increased with a further four albums. 2011's *Better Day* became her first Top 10 in the UK while 2014's *Blue Smoke* reached Number 2, coinciding with an appearance on the Sunday afternoon legend's slot at the Glastonbury Festival.

Album of the week: *Jolene*

Dolly Parton's thirteenth studio album *Jolene* was far from unlucky.

The album, which crams ten songs into just over twenty-five minutes, went on to sell over half a million records in the US.

Jolene includes her only UK Top 10 hit as a solo artist as well as future international hit "I Will Always Love You", which Whitney Houston took to the top of the world in 1992. The track was written as an ode to Porter Wagoner whose weekly TV series Parton had been appearing in for the previous seven years. In response, he penned the album's ninth track "Lonely Comin' Down".

The album signalled Dolly's departure to a solo career and her decision was justified. She wrote all but two tracks on the album which, although decidedly country sailed closely to the channels of pop music.

Dolly Parton continues to make music and in addition to her huge musical output has been lauded as an actor, starring in films such as *9 to 5* in 1980 and *Steel Magnolias* in 1989. She has also founded a number of charitable and philanthropic organisations including the Dollywood Foundation, which brings education and poverty relief to people across the United States, as well as the Imagination Library, which mails books every month to children across the country from birth until they reach kindergarten. She has also worked to raise money for several other causes including the American Red Cross and HIV/AIDS-related charities.

Your thoughts and reviews:

☆☆☆☆☆

Portishead

Portishead emerged from the British music scene in the early 1990s and quickly became a seminal force in trip-hop. Their sound blended elements of electronic music, jazz, hip-hop and rock while the combination of haunting vocals and innovative production techniques created an atmospheric sound that was both unique and compelling. Portishead remains a timeless and influential force in the world of alternative music, leaving an indelible mark on the genre and inspiring generations of musicians since.

Portishead formed in Bristol in 1991 when Beth Gibbins and Geoff Barrow met during the opulence of a coffee break while on an Enterprise Allowance course. It was probably the best thing to come out of the scheme, which promised £40 per week to unemployed people who set up their own businesses. The pair met Adrian Utley while recording their early work but despite co-producing debut album *Dummy*, playing instruments on nine of tracks and co-writing eight, the credits described Portishead at the time as the original duo of Gibbons and Barrow.

The group named themselves after the coastal town on the Severn Estuary ten miles from Bristol. It was the place where founding member Barrow had grown up and apparently hated, as anyone who has ever crossed the River Avon along the M5 and looked over the road barriers at the bleakness below will empathise with.

Similar artists:

Lamb
Massive Attack
Sneaker Pimps
Tricky

The band released *Dummy* in the summer of 1994 with "Glory Box", the final track on the album, receiving massive radio airplay that had disaffected teens and forty-something travelling salesman united in joyfully lamenting, "What in God's name is this?" towards their faceless DJs. It reached Number 13 as did the previous single "Sour Times" while the album peaked at Number 2, selling over three and a half million copies.

The following year *Dummy* won the Mercury Music Prize while the band also won Best International Dance/Rap Band at the Edison Awards and were nominated for Best Dance Act at the NME Awards, Best New Act at the MTV Europe Music Awards and British Breakthrough Act at the Brit Awards. This final nod was somewhat undone by the fact that PJ & Duncan also received a nomination.

The band followed up their success in 1997 with a self-titled album and again saw it reach Number 2. The record largely did away with the sampling that had proved so successful on *Dummy* while reaching for an even darker sound than their previous album, as if that were possible. The album spawned three Top 40 singles including the band's only Top 10 hit "All Mine". While fans and critics may have thought that *Portishead* was an unimaginatively titled album, eleven years later the band outdid themselves by naming third album *Third*. In the intervening years, Barrow had moved to Australia and despite efforts to create new music with Utley the results had proven futile.

Singled out:

"All Mine" – Brings forth images of a slow zombielike conga parade made up of every Scooby Doo baddie lined up to get their revenge on Velma while she searches in vain for her glasses.

"Glory Box" – Mid-1990s Britain was crying out for music to take a new direction and Bristol certainly delivered with its unique sound, unrecognisable and almost uncharacterisable.

"Roads" – A track incredible in its beauty and simplicity. It isn't true that the orchestral rise about 3:18 into the track is used to test for responses in coma patients but it could be.

Producing music for the Coral had reignited the pair's love of music and saw them team up once more with Gibbons, who had worked with Paul Webb in 2002 on the album *Out of Season*. *Third* proved to be Portishead's third and final album, peaking at Number 2, giving them a trio of silver medals.

In 2016 the band received an Ivor Novello Award for outstanding contribution to British music in the same year they released a cover of ABBA's "SOS". The last we heard of them was in 2022 when performing in their native Bristol in a concert for refugees and children affected by the Ukraine war.

Alongside other bands from their hometown, Portishead are often seen as the pioneers of the trip-hop genre (which has nothing to do with triple-hopped beer from Belgium). That they tried to distance themselves from this represented a confidence in their music that could have easily ridden on the coattails of their Bristolian contemporaries, however, this is understandable when you consider the sheer uniqueness of the sound they created.

Album of the week: *Dummy*

Portishead's debut album, released just one month ahead of Massive Attack's *Protection* and six months before Tricky's *Maxinquaye*, was timed perfectly to be the starting point of the trip-hop wave that spread from the Bristol Channel throughout the UK.

Singles "Sour Times" and "Glory Box" both peaked at Number 13 despite being gloriously radio unfriendly and impossible to categorise.

The album, which peaked at Number 2, went on to sell almost a million copies in the UK and over three and a half million worldwide.

In the years since, the sound of Portishead and their contemporaries has become ubiquitous yet at the time of release their music was like nothing else. The band didn't just sample records but rather manipulated the original recordings to the point where they were sliding on vinyl records, creating a sound so new that the word unique doesn't do it justice.

While Portishead's discography is relatively small compared to other bands, each release is a testament to their commitment to artistic integrity and innovation. Their influence extends beyond their own discography and they have inspired countless artists across various genres. Their impact on the music industry can still be felt today, with contemporary musicians acknowledging the band's importance to the evolution of electronic and alternative music.

Your thoughts and reviews:

☆☆☆☆☆

The Prodigy

Since forming in 1990 the Prodigy have revolutionised the music scene becoming a driving force behind electronic music's mainstream success at a time when it was still finding its footing. They were pioneers of the breakbeat-influenced big beat genre to emerge as one of the most successful electronic groups of all time. They sold over twenty-five million records worldwide, including over four and a half million albums in the UK alone, securing seven consecutive Number 1 albums along the way.

The Prodigy formed in Braintree, Essex, after musician and DJ Liam Howlett teamed up with dancers Keith Flint and Leeroy Thornhill at one of his gigs. The trio enlisted a fourth live member, female dancer and vocalist Sharky (no, not Feargal) who was a friend of Flint. The group later met MC Maxim and although he failed to attend an initial meeting he joined the group at their first gig. Sharky, meanwhile, left shortly after they signed their first record deal.

The band's debut EP *What Evil Lurks* initially bombed when first released in February 1991, however the record's fourth track "Everybody in the Place" would reach Number 2 when released as a single in December later that year. Prior to that, the band had achieved their first chart success in August with "Charly", which peaked at Number 3. Using samples from the well-known *Charley Says* series of TV adverts the single spawned several releases by other bands, termed 'toytown techno', that were in danger of making the Prodigy seem like a novelty act.

Similar artists:

The Chemical Brothers
Dutty Moonshine Big Band
Pendulum
Underworld

The band tended to avoid mainstream exposure and continued to do so throughout their career, with their reluctance to appear on TV programmes extending even as far as the BBC's stalwart *Top of the Pops*. Their performance of "Everybody in the Place" on the BBC2 music show *Dance Energy* remains their only live appearance on British television.

Debut album *Experience* was released in 1992, peaking at Number 12 and including the singles "Charly", "Everybody in the Place" and also Number 5 hit "Out of Space". A double A-side of singles "Fire" and "Jericho" was on a similar trajectory until it was pulled by the record label in order to give the album more focus. The album has since been considered a huge influence on the rave scene, inspiring many musicians at the time including a fledgling Moby.

The band followed up this success in 1994 with *Music for the Jilted Generation*, which saw a move away from their rave roots to adopt techno, breakbeat and rock influences while tackling themes including government corruption and social injustice in response to the Criminal Justice and Public Order Act 1994. The album entered the chart at Number 1 and all four of the singles released reached the Top 20 with "No Good (Start the Dance)" peaking at Number 4. Howlett only realised late on that the tracks were too long for one CD so edited several of the songs to shorten them while leaving out others completely. Despite this the record still runs to over seventy-eight minutes.

Singled out:

- "Out of Space" – Contains all the loops, bleeps, boings, beats and quacks along with a healthy image of a stranded Rastafarian astronaut to keep anyone happy.

- "Firestarter" – Singer Keith Flint bought an Essex pub and fined customers £1 if they cracked the Firestarter joke whenever he lit the open fire.

- "No Good (Start the Dance)" – The kind of thing you'd think and hope Beethoven would be producing if he was born in 1970 rather than 1770.

The Prodigy's third album, 1997's *The Fat of the Land*, went to Number 1 in sixteen countries and was the fastest-selling dance album at the time, eventually going on to sell more than ten million copies worldwide. It included Number 1 singles "Breathe" and "Firestarter", which was the first to feature Flint on vocals. Success came with controversy though and when the video for "Firestarter" was aired on *Top of the Pops* the BBC received its highest-ever number of complaints. With a hint of Bachman-Turner Overdrive's "You Ain't Seen Nothing Yet" in their ears, the band then released "Smack My Bitch Up", which was also slammed for both its incendiary lyrics and provocative video.

The fourth album *Always Outnumbered, Never Outgunned* again saw the band reach Number 1 although the single "Girls" was the only track to reach the Top 20. The following year their greatest hits album *Their Law: The Singles 1990–2005* sold almost one million copies in the UK alone. Their next three albums, released between 2009 and 2018, *Invaders Must Die*, *The Day Is My Enemy* and *No Tourists* all hit the top of the charts giving the band seven consecutive Number 1 albums in total.

Album of the week: *The Fat of the Land* [E]

Anticipation for the Prodigy's third studio album and the first to feature contributions from Keith Flint was high after the previous album *Music for a Jilted Generation* and singles promoting the album all reached Number 1.

Mired in controversy the third single from the album "Smack My Bitch Up" added to the band's notoriety but still reached the Top 10.

The album went on to sell over ten million copies worldwide.

As well as Flint, the album also sees appearances from Kula Shaker's Crispian Mills on the seventh track "Narayan" while being spiced up with the appearance of Saffron from Republica on the cover of L7's "Fuel My Fire".

The appeal spread across the world and saw the album reach Number 1 in the US while the band also played a free live show in Moscow's Red Square to over two hundred thousand Russians.

The charismatic Keith Flint was sadly found dead at his home in 2019 after taking his own life. His distinctive vocals and presence were integral to the Prodigy's later recordings while his death shone a huge spotlight on mental health issues faced particularly among men, bringing it into public discourse.

In 2022 the remaining members of the band went back out on tour and continued to do so throughout 2023.

Your thoughts and reviews:

☆☆☆☆☆

Minnie Riperton

Minnie Julia Riperton Rudolph's brief but illustrious career was cut short at the young age of just thirty-one years old. She was an American soul singer best known for her 1975 single "Lovin' You" and her vocal range that spanned five octaves and went into the whistle register, the highest phonational register created using only the back of the vocal folds. Despite the length of her career, Riperton's influence can still be heard in modern music with her unique voice style inspiring many contemporary artists including Beyoncé and Ariana Grande.

Minnie Riperton was born in Chicago in 1947. She was the youngest of eight children and demonstrated an early love of dance while her parents soon recognised her vocal abilities and encouraged her to explore a love of music. She was educated at the city's Abraham Lincoln Center where her incredible voice was further recognised while it was also here that she practised breathing and phrasing that would enable her to not only reach her incredibly high notes but also use them to sing coherently in a way that would set her apart from her contemporaries.

While at the Abraham Lincoln Center she received operatic vocal coaching and was later encouraged to study at Chicago's Junior Lyric Opera. Being young and more interested in soul, rhythm and blues and rock, Riperton had other ideas and after graduating from high school she enrolled at college but then later dropped out to pursue her music career.

Similar artists:

- Roberta Flack
- Phyllis Hyman
- Millie Jackson
- Evelyn 'Champagne' King

Riperton's first taste of professional singing came at the tender age of fifteen with a group called the Gems. They had little success although as a session group known as Studio Three, they did provide the backing vocals on 1965's "Rescue Me" by Fontella Bass. A year later she joined the funky rock-soul group Rotary Connection, releasing six albums between 1967 and 1971 while also being the backing band to Muddy Waters in 1968 and Howlin' Wolf in 1969. The group's most recognisable track "I Am the Black Gold of the Sun" came at the end of their career.

Debut solo album *Come to My Garden* was released in 1970 and while not commercially successful upon its release, peaking at Number 160 in the US, it has since been given the acclaim it deserves with the opening track "Les Fleurs" becoming particularly well-known.

After the relative failure of *Come to My Garden* Riperton went into semi-retirement to look after her two children. In 1973 however, a college intern for Epic Records heard a demo tape of her singing "Seeing You This Way" and played it to their bosses at the label who subsequently signed the singer.

Riperton's first album with Epic, *Perfect Angel*, featured the rock-soul anthem "Reasons" and "Take a Little Trip", the latter written by Stevie Wonder who also co-produced the album. Initial sales were disappointing until the release of the third single "Lovin' You", which catapulted Riperton to international stardom.

Singled out:

"You Take My Breath Away" – Minnie Riperton didn't just reach the high notes but sang lyrically within them. Here she is reaching her highest recorded note in the whistle register.

"Lovin' You" – Sounding like it comes straight from the voice of Snow White it's not just the birds tweeting in the background that make this sound like something out of a Disney film.

"Les Fleurs" – One of the singles that epitomise the very essence of the flower power generation, or in this case la production d'énergie florale.

The single was written by Riperton and husband Richard Rudolph as a lullaby to their daughter and was a fortuitous addition to the album, included at the last minute as Wonder wanted the LP to be closer to the forty-minute standard. With Riperton's vocals and Wonder on the keyboard, the song reached Number 2 in the UK, pushing the album to Number 33 and Number 4 in the US.

1975's *Adventures in Paradise* failed to chart in the UK but reached the US Top 20 and included the single "Inside My Love". The track was later covered by Trina Broussard, Chanté Moore and Delilah and sampled by DJ Jean Jacques Smoothie in his 2001 Number 21 hit "2 People". Riperton's fourth album *Stay in Love*, released in 1977, featured another collaboration with Stevie Wonder in the funky disco tune "Stick Together", however sales were again disappointing and in 1978 she orchestrated a move to Capitol Records. In 1979 she released her fifth album *Minnie,* which peaked at Number 29 in the US but failed to chart in the UK.

Album of the week: *Perfect Angel*

Minnie Riperton's second studio album was the only one of six to chart in the UK, peaking at Number 33. It also contained her only charting single, the Number 2 hit "Lovin' You." The eclectic nature of the album however made it difficult for it to gain momentum on US radio stations, which were dedicated to one type of music.

Perfect Angel was Riperton's first album released by Epic Records after the singer had taken a period of semi-retirement following her debut, *Come to My Garden*, released four years previously.

The record was co-produced by none other than Stevie Wonder, who was Riperton's first choice when asked.

As a fan Wonder agreed but had to do so under a pseudonym as he was contracted to Motown at the time.

Wonder co-produced the album, with Riperton's second choice, her husband Richard Rudolph, who hopefully didn't take offence at the minor sleight.

In January 1976, three years before the release of *Minnie*, Riperton had been diagnosed with breast cancer. Despite the prognosis and being given just six months to live she had continued recording and touring. She was one of the first celebrities to go public with a breast cancer diagnosis and in 1977 became a spokesperson for the American Cancer Society, receiving the American Cancer Society's Courage Award in 1978.

Riperton passed away on 12 July 1979 at the age of thirty-one. Her final album *Love Lives Forever* was released posthumously in 1980. The record, made up of vocals she'd recorded in 1978, stripped from their original tracks with new instrumentation added, reached the US Top 40.

Your thoughts and reviews:

Robyn

From early on in her career Robyn's success was characterised by her ability to blend infectious pop melodies with a distinctive voice that resonated with listeners. She navigated the unpredictable currents of the music industry with resilience and an unwavering commitment, evolving her sound as the musical landscape changed. Beyond her musical contributions she has made a mark as a fashion icon and an advocate for LGBTQ+ rights while her androgynous style and unapologetic approach to self-expression have resonated with fans who were drawn to her authenticity.

Born Robin Miriam Carlsson in Stockholm, Sweden, in 1979, Robyn's career in the music industry has encompassed singing, songwriting, producing and DJ roles. She enjoyed success at the tender age of just twelve when she recorded the theme tune "Du kan alltid bli nummer ett" ("You Can Always be Number One") for the children's sports programme *Lilla Sportspegeln* in 1991. She signed for Ricochet Records when she was just fourteen, having been spotted at a musical workshop at school by Swedish pop singer Meja.

At sixteen Robyn released her debut album *Robyn Is Here*, writing all the songs while co-writing "Do You Know (What It Takes)" with Herbie Crichlow and the Top 10 single "Show Me Love" with Max Martin. Martin would go on to enjoy enormous success, writing or co-writing twenty-five Billboard Hot 100 Number 1s, putting him in third place behind Paul McCartney and John Lennon.

Similar artists:

Bat For Lashes
La Roux
Goldfrapp
Röyksopp

Robyn's success started a clamour among music executives suddenly aware of a demand for white girls who could sing R&B. It paved the way for a flurry of similar artists such as Britney Spears, with record label bosses even referring to the "Oops!...I Did It Again" singer as an American Robyn.

While the follow-up album *My Truth* peaked at Number 2 in her native Sweden the record failed to chart elsewhere. Disillusioned with record label BMG over a lack of artistic control Robyn signed with Jive Records in 2001, however, a year later Jive was acquired by BMG and Robyn was back with her original label.

The third album, 2002's *Don't Stop the Music*, again peaked at Number 2 in Sweden while again failing to chart elsewhere. Two years later her record label's negative response to her new sound on "Who's That Girl" forced Robyn to leave and in 2005 she started her own. The decision and new sound proved successful with her next album *Robyn* reaching Number 11 in the UK. Three of the singles released reached the Top 20 while 2007's "With Every Heartbeat" peaked at Number 1.

In 2005 Robyn released a string of albums all within six months. *Body Talk Part 1*, featuring the Number 8 hit "Dancing on My Own" peaked at Number 47 when released in June, swiftly followed by *Body Talk Part 2* in September. By November people were getting a bit sick of body talk though and the final instalment in the trilogy stumbled in at Number 168.

Singled out:

"With Every Heartbeat" – The pulsating beat and build of the song make this an instant dancefloor hit while Robyn's hypnotically mournful lyrics add an element of melancholia to the party.

"Dancing On My Own" – The best songs are the ones we can relate to and we've all been the one in the corner at some point in our lives.

"Show Me Love" – Not to confused with "Show Me Love" by Robin S this catchy pop number comes from the time before Robyn set herself free from her record label to forge her own direction.

It would take a further eight years for Robyn to release her next album although she did release the EP *Do It Again* with fellow Scandinavians, Röyksopp in 2014, which reached Number 20. 2015's *Love Is Free*, produced with the magnificently named La Bagatelle Magique, fared less so, peaking at Number 111 while a 2017 collaboration with Mr Tophat titled *Trust Me* failed to chart.

Robyn's final and long-awaited album *Honey* was released in 2018, peaking just outside the Top 20 at Number 21. During the time away Robyn had to contend with the breakup with longtime collaborator Max Vitali and the death of close friend Christian Falk. This resulted in a long period of depression that brought out many of the traumas that Robyn had faced, both in her personal and professional life. The lead single from the album "Missing U" peaked at Number 87.

While not appearing as a solo artist since the release of *Honey*, Robyn did feature on the 2021 single "Times" by SG Lewis. In 2022 she then appeared on a remake of compatriot Nenah Cherry's remake of the 1988 classic "Buffalo Stance" for the singer's album *The Version*, which consists of reworked versions of songs from her back catalogue.

Album of the week: *Robyn* [E]

Robyn waited until her fourth album before making it eponymous.

Initially released only in Sweden and Norway in 2005, but given to the rest of the world throughout 2007 and 2008, the album featured six singles, four of which reached the Top 40. "Be Mine!" became a Top 10 hit while "With Every Heartbeat" reached Number 1.

The album peaked at Number 11 and sold almost a quarter of a million records in the UK alone.

Disillusioned with her record label forcing an R&B sound on previous albums, this was Robyn's first release under her own label. The move paid off and saw her first album since her debut *Robyn Is Here* chart outside of Sweden for the first time.

From a young age, one of Robyn's most significant accomplishments is her ability to connect with her audience on a profound emotional level. Her lyrics have delved into themes of love, heartbreak and self-discovery, creating a sense of intimacy that resonates with fans across the globe. This emotional authenticity, coupled with her dynamic stage presence and self-belief has endeared Robyn to a diverse and dedicated fan base throughout the world.

Your thoughts and reviews:

☆☆☆☆☆

Sigur Rós

Hailing from the enchanting land of Iceland the ethereal soundscapes and otherworldly compositions of **Sigur Rós** have forged a musical identity that is both mysterious and awe-inspiring. Their songs often start with delicate and atmospheric textures, gradually building up into powerful crescendos that evoke a sense of grandeur and beauty. The band's distinctive falsetto vocals sung in a language created by lead singer **Jón Þór Birgisson**, which he calls Hopelandic or Vonlenska, are unintelligible to listeners but still manage to convey raw emotion and allow the audience to interpret the songs in their own way.

Sigur Rós formed in Reykjavík in 1994 by Jón Þór 'Jónsi' Birgisson, Georg Hólm and Ágúst Ævar Gunnarsson. They were named Sigurrós, translated as victory rose, after Jonsi's sister who was born just before the band formed. They were joined in 1998 by Kjartan Sveinsson who, incredibly given the orchestral sound of the group, is the only member of Sigur Rós with any degree of musical training.

The band's debut album *Von* appeared in 1997 and while only released in Iceland it still managed to score a Number 33 hit in Germany. They followed this up in 1999 with *Ágætis byrjun* after which the band's reputation grew based on word of mouth and countless film and TV directors clamouring for the band's vivid songs to appear on their soundtracks. The album eventually reached Number 52 in the UK.

Similar artists:

Ólafur Arnolds
Explosions in the Sky
Lanterns on the Lake
Mogwai

Soon after the release of *Ágætis byrjun* Gunnarsson quit the group with Orri Páll Dýrason taking his place as the band's drummer. By this time they had become synonymous with Jónsi's vocal style along with their innovate use of a cello bow on guitars to create stunning reverberating resonances.

It was this distinctive sound that featured heavily on their highly-anticipated third album *()*, released in 2002. All tracks were initially untitled with the intention that listeners would come up with their own names while also encouraging them to write their own interpretations of the lyrics sung in the made-up language of Hopelandic. This is similar to how IKEA names its products. Titles were later added, with the album peaking at Number 49 and saw their first success in the US.

The fourth album *Takk*, released in 2005, continued with their trademark arrangements that conjured up images of vast landscapes, icy fjords and the raw power of nature. They continued to draw inspiration from the dramatic and breathtaking landscapes of their native Iceland, which is somewhat unsurprising given the terrain was used by NASA when training Neil Armstrong and Buzz Aldrin in preparation for them walking on the moon. *Takk* included their most recognisable track "Hoppípolla", which translates as hopping into puddles and was used relentlessly on TV promotions including the BBC's *Planet Earth* in 2006 and for numerous sports events. The single peaked at Number 24 with the album reaching Number 16.

Singled out:

"Hoppipolla" – That one from the telly. A track that screams the word finale, this could be the song they play at the world's end and you'd be able to find the beauty in Armageddon.

"Hljómalind" – Like travelling along on a sledge pulled along by huskies, gripping on tight to the person in front of you snow falls softly from Icelandic skies.

"Njósnavélin" – You can understand why the band left song titles and sleeve notes blank for listeners to come up with their own interpretations. This track means whatever you want it to mean.

In 2006 the band embarked on a major world tour with stops in Europe, North America, Australia, New Zealand, Hong Kong and Japan. Following this they returned to their native Iceland to provide a series of free outdoor concerts, playing in venues including abandoned bunkers and community coffee shops. These live recordings then formed the basis of their 2007 documentary *Heima* with the band's ability to recreate the intricate layers and sonic textures of their studio recordings in a live setting a testament to their musicianship and attention to detail.

2007 also saw the release of the compilation album *Hvarf/Heim*, with *Hvarf* containing studio versions of previously unreleased songs while *Heim* contained live acoustic versions of songs performed in the documentary. The album reached Number 23 in the UK with the single "Hljómalind" just creeping into the Top 100.

Album of the week: *()*

As with much of Sigur Rós's work the band wanted their listeners to interpret their sounds and aesthetics in their own way and so their third studio album was given the title of two brackets, allowing the listener to come up with their own title.

This ploy extended to the album booklet, which came with blank pages to allow listeners to complete their own thoughts and reflections on the music.

The album has since become known as *The Untitled Album*, which is annoying when searching on music streaming platforms. Alternatively it is also known as *The Bracket Album,* or *Svigaplatan* in their native Icelandic.

The album includes eight songs, initially untitled like the album but which have subsequently been given unofficial names.

The tracks are spread over seventy minutes, broken up by a thirty-six-second silence halfway through as if the band were yearning for the days of yore when you needed to flip the record.

The band's subsequent three studio albums all reached the Top 10. 2008's *Með suð í eyrum við spilum endalaust*, translated as *With a buzz in our ears we play endlessly*, was made available for free streaming and peaked at Number 5. 2012's *Valtari* reached Number 8, following which the band announced that Kjartan had left the band although he would later rejoin in 2022.

In 2013 they released *Kveikur* in a year they joined Johnny Cash, Dolly Parton and Lady Gaga, among many others, to have appeared on *The Simpsons*. A year later they appeared on *Game of Thrones*. The LP peaked at Number 9 and would be the band's last album for a decade before the release of *Átta* in 2023, which peaked at Number 30.

Your thoughts and reviews:

Nina Simone

Nina Simone was a complex and influential artist who not only produced some of the industry's most recognisable songs over a fifty-year career but whose impact transcended the boundaries of music. She emerged as a prominent figure and left an indelible mark on jazz, blues and soul. Simone possessed an unparalleled talent and distinctive voice while her unapologetic activism made her a symbol of empowerment and resilience throughout the last half of the 20th century. Her music continues to inspire and resonate with audiences worldwide while her courage in using her platform to address social and political issues remains a testament to the transformative power of music.

Nina Simone was born Eunice Kathleen Waymon in South Carolina in February 1933. She changed her name to Nina Simone once she started playing piano and singing in bars to pay for piano lessons and wanted to avoid being discovered by her deeply religious mother who referred to the music she was playing as Devil's music. The name Nina, Spanish for little one, was given to her by a boyfriend whereas Simone came from French actress Simone Signoret. She is also known as the High Priestess of Soul.

Simone was playing the piano by ear at the age of three, picking up the instrument (not physically) that stood in her mother's church. She signed a record deal at twenty-four and released her first album *Little Girl Blue* in 1959, which contained the US Top 20 hit "I Loves You, Porgy".

Similar artists:

Ella Fitgerald
Billie Holiday
Etta James
Sarah Vaughan

Little Girl Blue was the start of a career that resulted in over forty albums and spanned fifty years with her last studio album *A Single Woman* released in 1993. These studio recordings were remarkable while her live performances were captured on a number of releases that were the true testimony to Simone's prodigious talent. Her ability as a pianist and lyrical power and enunciation was unrivalled while being interspersed with a dry sense of humour, lamenting on the 1966 recording of "Mississippi Goddam" live in New York, "This is a show tune, but the show hasn't been written for it yet".

In 1965 Simone released the first of her albums to chart in the UK, *I Put a Spell on You*, which peaked at Number 18. The title track also gave Simone her first Top 50 hit. Three years later she released the singles "To Love Somebody", "Ain't Got No, I Got Life" and "Do What You Gotta Do" all of which reached the Top 5. Meanwhile album *'Nuff Said!* peaked at Number 11. Staggeringly these two would be the only studio albums that charted.

In addition to her music career, Nina Simone was a high-profile activist and spokesperson for the American civil rights movement. Her 1964 track "Mississippi Goddam" was banned in several southern states while she also covered Billie Holiday's "Strange Fruit" with lyrics that compare the victims of lynching to the fruit of trees. Other songs of social commentary included 1965's "Four Women" with each of the four women mentioned in the song representing an African American stereotype in society.

Singled out:

"Wild is the Wind" – You can almost picture leaves being blown about and umbrellas upended by Simone's lifting lyrics and progressive piano playing as this song reaches its crescendo.

"Feeling Good" – At first this appears as a lament of someone convincing themselves they're okay yet soon turns into a rousing challenge to anyone or anything that wants to stop her on the rise.

"My Baby Just Cares for Me" – Originally recorded in 1957 this became a Top 10 hit in 1987 after being used in a perfume commercial, resulting in a sweet-smelling renaissance.

Simone's conviction was shaped by many acts that she experienced throughout her life, some dating into her early years. At her first piano recital at the age of twelve her parents were told to move from the seats they had taken in the front row of the concert hall in favour of white people, after which Nina Simone refused to play until they were allowed back into their seats.

Later, in 1951, she auditioned for a scholarship to attend Philadelphia's prestigious Curtis Institute of Music but was rejected. This, she maintained, was down to pure and simple racism and it's a testament to Simone, along with the great many people who campaigned for civil rights throughout the century, that the institute would later grant her an honorary degree.

Simone was also deeply affected by the murder of the American civil rights activist Medgar Evers in 1963 and the 16th Street Baptist Church bombing of the same year. This took the lives of four young girls, fourteen-year-olds Addie Mae Collins, Carole Rosamond Robertson and Cynthia Dionne Wesley as well as Carol Denise McNair, age just eleven.

Album of the week: *'Nuff Said!*

All but three of the tracks featured on Nina Simone's *'Nuff Said!* album were recorded at the Westbury Music Fair on 7 April 1968, just three days after the murder of Dr. Martin Luther King Jr.

The evening was dedicated to his memory and therefore these recordings were particularly poignant for Simone after her lifelong support of the civil rights movement.

The sixth track, "Why? (The King of Love Is Dead)" was penned by Simone's bass player Gene Taylor as soon as he heard the news.

The album, released six months after the Westbury fair, also featured studio versions of a cover of the Bee Gees' "In the Morning" and two of Simone's biggest-ever hits "Do What You Gotta Do" and "Ain't Got No, I Got Life" both of which reached Number 2. The album peaked at Number 11 in the UK.

Nina Simone continued to use her platform in support of the civil rights movement despite knowing this would damage a musical career that should have yielded far richer rewards. This is all the more reason to be inspired by this wonderful musician and her integrity.

Nina Simone passed away peacefully in her sleep in April 2003.

Your thoughts and reviews:

☆ ☆ ☆ ☆ ☆

Dusty Springfield

Dusty Springfield enjoyed a career that spanned over thirty years but it was the 1960s that saw her heyday when she ranked among the most successful British female performers. Her success was found in her native UK but she was also at the forefront of the first British invasion – a term which has been used sporadically anytime there is a glut of music from Britain invading the US Charts. Springfield saw eighteen singles hit the Billboard Hot 100 from 1964 to 1970 including six in the Top 20.

Dusty Springfield was born Mary Isobel Catherine Bernadette O'Brien in London in 1939. She was known as Dusty as she was often found playing football with boys in the street. In 1958 she had a brief stint with the Lana Sisters before going on to form the Springfields in 1960 with her brother Tom (originally called Dion) and Tim Field. On Field's advice, the group adopted the name to appear familiar to audiences in the US with an abundance of places by the name of Springfield across the country. This was a similar tactic employed by Matt Groening when deciding to locate *The Simpsons* in 1989.

It was here that Dusty demonstrated the first inclinations of her intense attention to detail, lining up the trio in front of the mirror for hours to practice their onstage routine. The group enjoyed five Top 40 hits between 1961 and 1963 including "Islands of Dreams" and "Say I Won't Be There" both of which reached Number 5. 1962's "Silver Threads and Golden Needles" also reached the US Top 20 becoming the first single by a British group to do so.

Similar artists:

Petula Clark
Jojo Effect
Gloria Jones
Sandie Shaw

Wanting to distance herself from the folk sound of the Springfields and also her brother's lead role within the band Dusty decided to quit with the group announcing their split on *Sunday Night at the London Palladium* in October 1963. Her solo career was an instant success just a month later with the November release of her debut single "I Only Want to Be with You" eventually reaching Number 4 the following January, a feat achieved in no small part to it being the first song aired on *Top of the Pops* when the programme launched on 1 January that year.

Dusty Springfield recorded a total of ten albums throughout the 1960s often alternating between releases in the UK and the US. Of the four UK albums debut *A Girl Called Dusty* and 1965's *Ev'rything's Coming Up Dusty* both peaked at Number 6. She also released sixteen Top 40 singles throughout the 1960s, ten of which reached the Top 10 and included the Number 1 hit "You Don't Have to Say You Love Me".

As well as her own music Springfield is also credited as bringing the sound of Motown to the UK during the 1960s. She often covered songs from the music label while inviting artists such as the Temptations, the Supremes and Stevie Wonder to record their first UK TV appearances on her TV show *Ready Steady Go!* She also helped launch the career of Led Zeppelin by suggesting to Jerry Wexler of Atlantic Records that he should sign the band, having known bass guitarist John Paul Jones from his session work with her.

Singled out:

"I Only Want to Be with You" – Regaling the simplicity of love in a decade when everything was as easy as jelly and ice cream, Morris Minors and England winning the men's football World Cup.

"Son of a Preacher Man" – One of those euphonic phrases that roll off the tongue like cellar door, the phonaesthetic sound of son of a preacher man made the single a success before it was sung.

"You Don't Have to Say You Love Me" – This song erupts in a cacophony of intense orchestral sound that makes you wonder how any singer could begin to compete with it.

While her distinctive soulful, sultry voice was her trademark Springfield was also very outspoken when it came to issues of race and sexuality, standing steadfast in her beliefs even when they damaged her career. In December 1964 a tour of South Africa was terminated when she performed in front of an integrated audience of black and white people at a theatre near Cape Town, which was in defiance of the government's segregation policy. Her contract specifically excluded segregated performances making her one of the first British artists to do so.

Springfield was also open about her bisexuality and was a trailblazer for LGBTQ+ representation in the music industry. After coming out in an interview with the London Standard in 1970 her career was hit hard and of the five albums released that decade only *A Brand New Me* and *It Begins Again* reached the charts while the single "How Can I Be Sure?" was the only one to reach the Top 40.

Album of the week: *Dusty in Memphis*

Despite selling poorly on release and initially hated by the artist herself *Dusty in Memphis* has since grown in acclaim.

It was the singer's fifth UK release and only third track "Son of a Preacher Man" charted in the UK, reaching Number 9. The album failed to chart in the UK and just hit the US Top 100 at 99.

Springfield's desire to earn more credibility by signing to Atlantic Records backfired as she became increasingly intimidated working in studios graced by celebrated singers of the past, which she failed to believe she could emulate. Subsequently recordings were difficult and wracked with indecision.

The album did spawn a run of ...*in Memphis* albums for Atlantic though, which would go on to feature Dionne Warwick, Petula Clark and Elvis Presley.

It was also during these sessions that Springfield convinced executives at Atlantic to sign Led Zeppelin, so not a complete waste of time then.

Hounded by the British press Springfield fled to the United States. Her career was somewhat revived in 1987 though when she teamed up with Pet Shop Boys on the single "What Have I Done to Deserve This?". Her 1990 album *Reputation* was her first in the UK since 1979 and peaked at Number 18 while boasting three Top 40 singles. Her music then reached a new audience in 1994 when her 1968 hit "Son of a Preacher Man" featured on the *Pulp Fiction* soundtrack.

Dusty Springfield died of breast cancer in Henley-on-Thames in March 1999, a month before her sixtieth birthday. It was the same year she was inducted into the Rock and Roll Hall of Fame.

Your thoughts and reviews:

☆☆☆☆☆

The Strokes

The Strokes burst onto the music scene in the early 2000s with their distinctive blend of garage rock, post-punk revival and catchy melodies. Their early sound containing raw production and unapologetic rock attitude set them apart from the polished pop music of the time and paved the way for a new wave of garage rock revivalists including bands such as the Killers, Arctic Monkeys and Kings of Leon.

Lead singer and songwriter Julian Casablancas, guitarist Nick Valensi and drummer Fabrizio Moretti all started playing music together as teenagers while at Dwight School in Manhattan. They later added bassist Nikolai Fraiture, a close friend of Casablancas and invited guitarist Albert Hammond Jr. who Casablancas had met while at boarding school in Switzerland to join at the end of 1998. Hammond came with all the pedigree of an obese dog with his father having penned a number of hits including the Hollies' "Air That I Breathe" and Whitney Houston's "One Moment in Time".

The band first played as the Strokes in September 1999 and sent their first demo tape, which contained "The Modern Age", "Last Nite" and "Barely Legal", to the newly formed Rough Trade Records label the following year. Their first release, the instantly catchy "Last Nite", came in 2001 via a free MP3 download in the music magazine NME a week before they released the demo as an EP. A bidding war then ensued after which the band signed to RCA Records.

Similar artists:

Franz Ferdinand
Interpol
Jet
The Killers

The band released their debut album *Is This It* (minus the question mark) in the summer of 2001. It peaked at Number 2 selling over half a million copies in the UK and over one million in the US. This came despite delays in the record due to the controversial track "New York City Cops" having to be changed in the US with the release coming in the wake of the September 11 attacks. The front cover, which depicted the photographer's naked girlfriend in semi-profile also had to be replaced in their native land.

The band followed *Is This It* in 2003 with *Room on Fire*, which spawned their first Top 10 single "12:51". Sales-wise the album was less successful than their debut but still reached Number 2 in the UK and Number 4 in the US whereas their previous album had schlepped in at Number 33.

Ahead of the 2005 album *First Impressions of Earth*, the single "Juicebox" was leaked online but despite this it still became the band's second UK Top 10 hit, while the album became their first and only Number 1. They followed this up in 2006 with eighteen sold-out shows during a tour of the UK.

After a five-year hiatus, the band returned with *Angles* in 2011 and *Comedown Machine* in 2013. The albums incorporated elements of new wave, synth-pop and electronica and while *Angles* peaked at Number 3 *Comedown Machine* was true to its word and saw dwindling sales. This wasn't helped by the band pulling a media blackout due to in-house fighting resulting in no TV appearances, interviews, photoshoots, shows or tours taking place.

Singled out:

"12:51" – Melodic and lovely with a playful keyboard sound that overcomes the deadpan vocals of Julian Casablancas to the point of lullaby.

"Last Nite" – Everybody on the planet knows the opening four words to this song. Fewer know the following twenty-eight but we all pick it up for the final ten before the next verse comes along.

"The Adults Are Talking" – A track that sounds like one dog on the planet got the ability to speak and was deep in conversation while all other dogs contributed thinking they'd been given the same gift.

The band members spent much of the following years working on solo projects but in 2019 performed for the first time in over two years, kickstarting a global comeback tour. Unfortunately sound issues, festival cancellations and thunderstorms all had a detrimental effect.

The following year they returned to the studio releasing their sixth studio album *The New Abnormal*. The album put them back in the media's good books and secured a high of Number 3 in the UK and a Top 10 spot in the US while also winning Best Rock Album at the sixty-third Annual Grammy Awards.

Album of the week: *Is This It* [E]

The Strokes released their debut album, produced in just six weeks on Julian Casablancas' insistence they create something raw, across the world at various times throughout 2001 to coincide with the band's touring schedule.

Lead single "Hard to Explain" reached Number 16 ahead of the album release with singles "Last Nite" and "Someday" peaking at Number 14 and Number 27 respectively.

The album peaked at Number 2 but bizarrely missed the mark in their native US, peaking at Number 33 although did end up selling over one million copies, which contributed to sales of over two million worldwide.

The album title appears without the question mark as the band didn't think it looked right. It was also beset with trouble in the US with the cover featuring the profile of a woman's gloved hand on her bare butt deemed sexually explicit and replaced with subatomic particle tracks in a bubble chamber, none of which I understand. Stores in England were also unhappy but stocked it anyway.

More understandable was the CD release being subsequently delayed from September 25 to October 9 while they replaced "New York City Cops" in light of the attacks on the city's World Trade Center.

The band toured throughout 2022 with headline slots at Lollapalooza in South America and festivals across Europe. They also supported the Red Hot Chilli Peppers on their *Global Stadium* tour, by the way.

Two decades after they burst onto the scene the Strokes' legacy persists with subsequent generations of musicians citing them as a significant influence. They not only revived rock music but also reminded us of the enduring power of a straightforward, unapologetic and authentic approach to music.

Your thoughts and reviews:

☆☆☆☆☆

Sister Rosetta Tharpe

Sister Rosetta Tharpe, the Godmother of Rock and Roll, gained popularity across the United States in the 1930s and 1940s with her brand of music that was the first to span spiritual and secular audiences. She took gospel music from the church and into nightclubs and concert halls, blending spiritual lyrics and the electric guitar characterised by intricate fingerpicking, soulful slides and a distinct, percussive style, which set her apart from her contemporaries. She was also among the first artists to use heavy distortion, opening the way for electric blues that would later become the precursor to rock and roll.

Born Rosetta Nubin in Cotton Plant, Arkansas, in 1915, Sister Rosetta Tharpe's mother was the first to recognise her early genius and encouraged her at the age of six to play the guitar and sing. She took her daughter along to perform concerts that were part sermon and part gospel before audiences across the southern states of America as a member of the Church of God in Christ whose formation in the latter stages of the 19th century jumped on the bandwagon of the emergence of gospel music by encouraging praise through music and dancing.

At the age of nineteen Rosetta married Thomas Thorpe and although the marriage lasted only a few years she adopted a version of her husband's name to become Sister Rosetta Tharpe. Although she married several times she performed as Rosetta Tharpe for the rest of her life.

Similar artists:

Memphis Minnie
Odetta
Ma Rainey
Big Mama Thornton

In 1938 at the age of twenty-three Tharpe became the first gospel singer to record for a major label when she signed to Decca Records to produce "Rock Me, That's All", "My Man and I" and "The Lonesome Road". All were instant hits making Tharpe one of the first commercially successful gospel recording artists. Her success however was not universally popular with many unhappy with her mixing the gospel-based lyrics with secular music.

In 1945 "Strange Things Happening Every Day" featuring Tharpe's now familiar blend of vocal and resonator guitar became the first gospel song to enter the US charts. It is also widely regarded as the first rock and roll record ever made.

Tharpe released her first album *Gospel Songs* in 1947, followed up four years later in 1951 with *Blessed Assurance.* The following year, along with country and western star Red Foley, she broke further new ground when they recorded "Have a Little Talk with Jesus". The song is thought to be the first interracial duet recorded in the US and could have easily been titled "Have a Little Word with Yourselves".

In 1956 Tharpe recorded her third album *Gospel Train*, moving her to a more jazz-based sound, which was followed by a month-long tour to the UK. Three years later Tharpe would hit a purple patch in terms of recording, releasing five albums in the space of three years although *The Gospel Truth* was released twice during this time.

Singled out:

"Strange Things Happening Every Day" – Said to be the first rock and roll record and with an instantly recognisable piano blazing in the background, this was a precursor to all that came after.

"Up Above My Head, I Hear Music in the Air" – The call and return make for an easy singalong to this perfect blend of gospel and rock and roll.

"When They Ring the Golden Bell" – A song essentially about what happens at the time of death but performed with such optimism it's like the stairway to heaven is taken via a walk along Brighton Pier.

In 1964 Tharpe brought her music to Europe as part of the Blues and Gospel Caravan tour performing alongside Muddy Waters and Otis Spann. One show in particular at a disused railway station at Wilbraham Road in Manchester in May of that year was attended by rock royalty including Eric Clapton, Jeff Beck, Keith Richards and Brian Jones. It is said to have had a similar influential effect as that of the Sex Pistols' 1976 show at Manchester's Lesser Free Trade Hall, which saw Morrissey, Mark E Smith, Joy Division and all Buzzcocks aspire to be musicians.

Tharpe suffered a stroke in 1970 and as a result, her performances were severely curtailed. Three years later she suffered another stroke and passed away on the eve of a scheduled recording session. She was fifty-eight years old.

Album of the week: *Gospel Train*

Gospel Train was Sister Rosetta Tharpe's third album and the first to be released after the formation of the UK Charts in July 1956.

The LP sees her move to a more jazz-based sound and away from the innovative rock and roll and blues from which she made her name.

Tharpe composed all but ten of the twelve tracks on the album, which are crammed into just over thirty-two minutes of music with song titles that point to her religious nature and fly in the face of rock and roll as being the Devil's music.

"When They Ring the Golden Bell" presents a jaunty optimistic view of the journey to heaven, if you believe that kind of thing, as is the spirit of "Can't No Grave Hold My Body Down". Meanwhile seventh track "Up Above My Head, I Hear Music in the Air" was originally recorded by Tharpe in 1947, nine years before this release. It would later be recorded in 1964 as a duet by Long John Baldry and Rod Stewart as Long John Baldry and the Hoochie Coochie Men, presumably because Baldry wouldn't be seen dead singing along with Rod Stewart.

Sister Rosetta Tharpe will be remembered for pushing spiritual music into the mainstream, helping to push the evolution of gospel music into R&B and rock and roll. As well as those present at her Manchester concert in 1964 she is also said to have been a major influence on Elvis Presley, Johnny Cash, Chuck Berry and Jerry Lee Lewis. Tharpe was also responsible for giving Little Richard his first paid job as a singer, leading him to become the performer that he was and therefore responsible for all who he influenced as well.

Your thoughts and reviews:

Toots and the Maytals

Known originally as just the Maytals when formed in 1962, riding on the crest of hope after Jamaican independence the group added the Toots (for want of a better expression) after frontman Frederick 'Toots' Herbert a decade later. Over a career spanning six decades and twenty-four studio albums, the group became one of the best-known reggae vocal groups across the world. They were key figures in not only popularising reggae music but also coining the term after their 1968 single "Do the Reggay". They currently hold the record of Number 1 hits in Jamaica with a total of thirty-one.

The original trio of Frederick 'Toots' Hibbert, Henry 'Raleigh' Gordon and Nathaniel 'Jerry' Mathias called themselves the Maytals after the Jamaican word for good things, with Maytals themselves referring to the people who bring those good things.

'Toots' was born in 1942 and grew up singing gospel music in church before moving to Kingston in the late 1950s. His contribution to Jamaican music is on par with Bob Marley, his soulful vocal style has been compared to Otis Redding while Rolling Stone magazine has listed him as being one of the one hundred greatest singers of all time.

The original trio to make up the band met at a barber's shop in Jamaica's capital city in 1962. Originally a vocal trio the group expanded when they signed with Island Records and incorporated their recording band.

Similar artists:

Jimmy Cliff
Desmond Decker
The Heptones
The Skatalites

The Toots and the Maytals sound was characterised by Hibbert's powerful vocals and backed by a tight and infectious rhythm section. Their music blends elements of ska, rocksteady and reggae creating a unique and dynamic sound that has inspired countless musicians not only in their native Jamaica but around the world.

The band started prolifically and in 1963 released a torrent of eight singles along with three shared singles, upon which another artist recorded a track for the other side. The following year they released twenty tracks along with nine that followed the shared single format. They also managed to release their debut album *Never Grow Old* that year.

This debut album was followed up a year later with *The Sensational Maytals*, after which the group were forced into a period out of the spotlight when Hibbert was jailed for eighteen months. This could have been the end of the band but they emerged stronger with Hibbert having penned one of the group's best-known tracks "54-46 That's My Number" while in jail.

Following Hibbert's incarceration the band released the single "Do the Reggay" in 1968. This was the first to reference the style of music that the band, along with others, had been releasing since the early part of the decade and a whole new genre was born. A year later they released the album *Sweet and Dandy* followed swiftly by the magical *Monkey Man*, which was their first release on the legendary Trojan Records.

Singled out:

- "Pressure Drop" – The sunshine of this track simply streams through the windows and into your heart with soulful gospel backing vocals that raise it even higher.

- "Monkey Man" – Resurrected by both the Specials and Amy Winehouse, the charm of the relatively rudimentary nature of the original recording is undeniable.

- "54-46 That's My Number" – The incessant bassline, which has been copied countless times, is the perfect vehicle for Hibbert's tuneful voice that you can't fail to be moved by.

In 1972 the group came to international attention after contributing two songs to the soundtrack for *The Harder They Come*. The records introduced Jamaican music to American and European audiences, popularising the style of music and taking it further than the Jamaican shores.

Later, in 1975, they released the compilation album *Funky Kingston*, which reached the Top 200 in the US while also supporting the Who on a tour that included playing to a crowd of ninety thousand people in California.

During the latter part of the decade, the band experienced a resurgence as part of a reggae, punk and ska revival across the UK. "Pressure Drop" was released by the Clash in 1979 as the B-side to their Number 25 hit single "English Civil War" while the Specials covered "Monkey Man" on their eponymous 1979 debut album. The single was further popularised in 2006 after being recorded by Amy Winehouse and included on the bonus disc of her Number 1 hit album *Back to Black*.

Album of the week: *Monkey Man*

Toots and the Maytals fourth studio album, and the first to be released on the Trojan record label that would later partner Bob Marley and the Wailers, contains no less than twenty-six tracks of early reggae to feast your ears on.

The title single was their first and one of few songs to chart when recorded by themselves, reaching Number 47 when released prior to the album in 1969.

Other singles from the album include "Sweet and Dandy" and "Bla Bla Bla" while they also released split singles, sharing the records with other artists. "Peeping Tom" and "One Eye Enos" were released with versions by Beverley's All Stars on the B-side while "Pressure Drop", the song that brought the band international attention after featuring on the soundtrack to the 1972 film *The Harder They Come*, was released with the Beverley's All Stars' adding their own song "Smoke Screen".

The group subsequently split after releasing the 1981 album *Knockout*, however in the early 1990s a new line-up of the Maytals was formed. Following the death of 'Toots' in September 2020 there was uncertainty over whether the band would continue but by November they confirmed that they would continue as a tribute. 'Toots'' family disagreed however and in July 2021 they prohibited the band from performing under the name.

Your thoughts and reviews:

Amy Winehouse

Despite an incredibly short career, the sound of Amy Winehouse captured the world with her powerful voice, unique style and deeply personal lyrics. Her eclectic blend of soul, R&B, reggae and jazz was an antidote to the formulaic stream of reality TV celebrities of the day as she fearlessly delved into themes of love, heartbreak, addiction and personal struggles. She became the first British woman to win five Grammys while her two albums sold over nineteen million records worldwide.

Amy Winehouse was born in London in 1983. Her initiation into jazz music came at an early age via many of her uncles who were professional jazz musicians while her grandmother had dated the legendary Ronnie Scott. It was her grandmother who suggested she attend theatre school where Winehouse developed her vocals while also learning to tap dance.

The singer bought her first guitar when she was just fourteen and began writing her own music soon after. At the age of nineteen she signed to Simon Fuller's 19 Management and released her first album *Frank* in 2003 just a month after her twentieth birthday. All but one of the album's tracks were co-written by Winehouse herself although the four singles released failed to reach the Top 50. By January 2004 however, the album itself was proving a success and had climbed to Number 13 in the charts. It charted again after her death in 2011, peaking at Number 3 and has since sold over a million copies in the UK and three million worldwide.

Similar artists:

- Duffy
- Etta James
- Janis Joplin
- Nina Simone

Winehouse's attention to detail was incredible. During the production of her second album *Back to Black* she would record early versions on a CD to be played in her dad's taxi to enable her to experience how her listeners would hear the songs. The album was released in 2006, peaking at Number 1 in January of the following year and becoming the best-selling album of 2007. The album also spawned five Top 40 singles with "Rehab" and "Back to Black" both reaching the Top 10.

After success at the Grammys in 2008, which yielded no fewer than five awards for the singer-songwriter, sales of *Back to Black* rapidly increased in the US making it a Number 2 hit and prompting a deluxe edition that again topped the charts. The album eventually sold over four million copies in the UK, three million in the US and over sixteen million across the world.

Winehouse was still only twenty-three years of age but despite her immense talent and success she was also battling personal demons that plagued her throughout her short career. Substance abuse, eating disorders and mental health issues took their toll on her wellbeing with her struggles often played out in a frenzied media and onstage. A string of live performances were cancelled but her battle against the paparazzi was won when she took them to court, resulting in a ban on her being followed. All this led to a level of notoriety that, coupled with her emotional lyrics and musical style, added to the attention placed upon her.

Singled out:

"Back to Black" [E] – The minor chords instantly transform you into a place as dark as where Winehouse was when she penned this track before the tuneful chorus appears to pull you from the abyss.

"Rehab" – A tragically prophetic anthem with an almost joyful cocktail of instruments, masking the darker side of the lyrics that hint at the oppressive men surrounding her life.

"Tears Dry on Their Own" [E] – The unmistakable nod to Northern Soul makes this track inevitably catchy, demonstrating the singer's ability not only to replicate the sounds of the past but better them.

Amy Winehouse's last public appearance took place in London at Camden's Roundhouse on 20 July 2011 when she appeared on stage to support her Goddaughter Dionne Bromfield. She died three days later. Following her death the compilation album *Lioness: Hidden Treasures* was issued featuring unreleased songs, covers and demos. It peaked at Number 1 in the UK and sold three-quarters of a million copies.

What was largely unnoticed throughout her career, mainly as it didn't fit the narrative of the tortured artist, was Winehouse's commitment throughout her career to charitable causes, in particular those concerned with children. She appeared naked in an issue of *Easy Living* magazine to raise awareness of breast cancer and contributed music to a CD to raise awareness of climate change. She once donated over £20,000 worth of clothes to a local charity shop and even paid £4,000 for a patient's urgent surgery during a stay in Saint Lucia.

Album of the week: *Back to Black* [E]

Five of the eleven tracks on Amy Winehouse's second and final album became hit records, two of which, "Rehab" and "Back to Black" reached the Top 10.

The opening line of "Rehab" was born from a conversation with producer Mark Ronson in a New York park, who thought the admission was catchy, totally missing the point of what turned out to be a prophetic warning. Meanwhile her vocals on his version of the Zutons' "Valerie", which the band took to Number 9 in 2006, peaked at Number 2.

Reading the titles of each track is enough to instil a sense of melancholy and give an insight into the troubled mind of the singer at the time, who either wrote or co-wrote all songs on the album.

Initially the album was kept off the top of the charts by Girls Aloud and Robbie Williams, but soon hit Number 1 in the UK and elsewhere across the globe. The album went on to sell over four million records in the UK alone and sixteen million worldwide.

But first and foremost it was the powerful lyrics and voice of Amy Winehouse that set her apart from her contemporaries while her attitude to promoting her music and image in a male-dominated industry opened the doors for future female artists including strong independent females such as Lady Gaga, Adele, Paloma Faith, Lana Del Rey, Florence Welch and Billie Eilish. Meanwhile her struggles, which in hindsight are so visible now, have put the mental health of performers high on an agenda that never existed in her day, prolonging careers that, like in Winehouse's case, could have otherwise been cruelly cut short.

Your thoughts and reviews:

☆ ☆ ☆ ☆ ☆

Acknowledgements

A huge amount of gratitude is due to Jane Harris for her unwavering and unconditional support throughout the writing process. Without her enthusiasm for the book it would have stumbled along the way many times.

Eternal thanks and praise are also due to Darren Pyefinch whose infectious love for music ignited my own passion for finding my all-time favourite song.

Thank you to Jon Randle for taking the time to proofread the book and also to the hugely creative Scott Hingley for designing the cover and coming up with the inspired title.

Finally, a huge thanks to all the family and friends who greeted this project with a genuine sense of excitement as to how it would turn out – there are too many to name, but if at some point you told me it was a great idea, you have my gratitude too.

Also by the author:

Son of My Father: Me, My Dad and Derby County

To the backdrop of driving through clouds to Oldham to driving rain in Bristol, Son of My Father explores the changing relationship between father, son and their football club.

From the eyes of a hero-worshipping four-year-old through to a relationship of mutual admiration and shared understanding via the angst and traumatic misunderstandings of an adolescent, matches from Leyton to Liverpool punctuate a story about growing up at the end of the second millennium.

The novel includes the family life as well as the football and what it was like supporting Derby County in a house occupied by a brother whose allegiance stood steadfast towards rivals Nottingham Forest. It also covers the friendships that were made at school just because we supported the same team.

Along with the changing faces of managers and players the fads, news and music of the eighties and nineties are brought to life as well as the dawning of the new millennium where overnight we all realised that despite the Y2K Bug promising computer meltdown, 1 January 2000 was just the same as 31 December 1999.